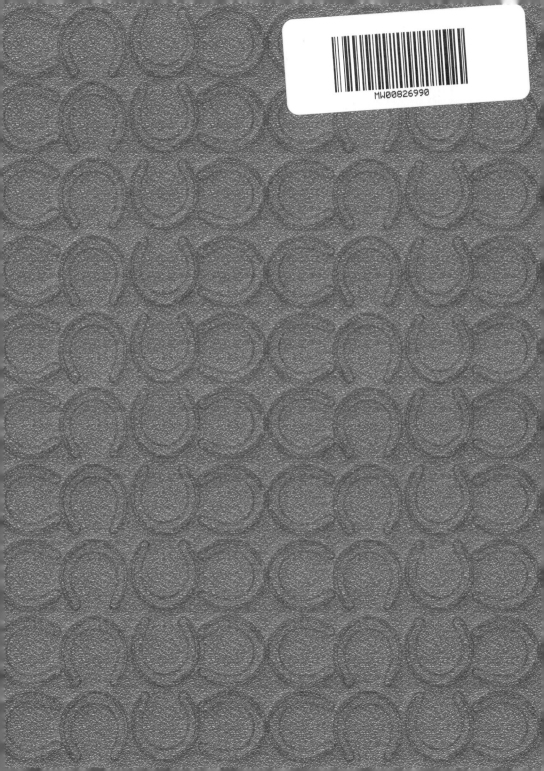

Sunday Silence

Sunday Silence

by RAY PAULICK

THOROUGHBRED
Legends®
No. 12

Lexington, Kentucky

Library of Congress Control Number: 2001090252

ISBN 1-58150-061-0

Printed in The United States
First Edition: December 2001

a division of
The Blood-Horse, Inc.
PUBLISHERS SINCE 1916

To learn more about Sunday Silence
and other classic Thoroughbreds, see:

www.thoroughbredlegends.com

CONTENTS

Introduction 6
Horse Of Destiny
Chapter 1 10
Praying For A Miracle
Chapter 2 24
Providential
Chapter 3 40
A Tough Sell
Chapter 4 56
"Sunday Stop It"
Chapter 5 70
No Easy Rival
Chapter 6 80
Rolling The Dice
Chapter 7 94
Silent No More
Chapter 8 112
R-E-S-P-E-C-T
Chapter 9 128
Easy Does It
Chapter 10 144
Who's Best?
Chapter 11 156
"Much The Best"
Chapter 12 174
Sayonara Sunday
Chapter 13 192
Best In The World
Epilogue 202
Rivalry Enshrined

Pedigree 206
Past Performances 207
Index 208
Photo Credits 214
About the Author 215

INTRODUCTION

Horse Of Destiny

On Thanksgiving Day in 1986, the staff at Stone Farm looked forward to an easy day and an early dinner. But a little black colt interfered with their plans.

Stricken with diarrhea, the eight-month-old youngster struggled for his life. He was the only one of the nearly 140 Thoroughbred foals born on the Paris, Kentucky, farm that year to come down with the illness.

Despite being sick, the colt aroused little sympathy.

Sired by the farm's top stallion, Halo, and produced from a broodmare named Wishing Well, the colt stood out from the pack, but for all the wrong reasons. He was sickly, thin, and his hind legs were put together in a way that made horsemen grimace — the hocks, the large joints in the back legs that appear to bend backwards, curved inward to the point they almost touched. The condition was known as sickle hocked, since the legs were curved in the shape of a sickle. These were not the kind of legs that were expected to carry a Thoroughbred racehorse at speeds of up to forty miles per hour.

Along with all that, the colt had an uncooperative attitude probably inherited from Halo, who would savagely attack his handlers for no apparent reason.

So the little black colt may not have received an overabundance of tender care when he got sick on November 27, 1986. Farm staff attended to him, including the resident veterinarian, Carl Morrison, who knew his job was to do everything in his power to save the horse. The walls of the colt's stall were lined with evidence of the diarrhea that left him severely dehydrated. Morrison pumped liter after liter of fluids into the sick horse, monitoring him throughout the day, well past the hour when most families had sat down to enjoy their Thanksgiving dinner.

Finally, after the twenty-third liter of fluid had been given intravenously to the colt, Morrison's frustrations came to a boil. He had had enough. "If you're going to, why don't you just go on and die now, you little son of a bitch," a tired Morrison said. "I'm hungry."

Arthur B. Hancock III, the owner of Stone Farm, later

would look back at that Thanksgiving Day and have a better understanding why that sickly, black colt survived the serious illness and grew to become one of the twentieth century's great Thoroughbred champions.

That colt, Sunday Silence, was a fighter. "You have to have a lot of heart to live through something like that," Hancock said. "He proved something to me that day. That same determination, which can only come from inside, is what made him such a great racehorse."

The illness that nearly killed Sunday Silence was only his first obstacle. Over the next two years, before he ever set foot on a racetrack, Sunday Silence endured a long string of insults and setbacks. His breeder, acting on the advice of a handful of advisers and world-renowned trainers, didn't want to keep him and Hancock wound up buying him, almost by default. Buyers at public auction twice shrugged an indifferent shoulder at the colt. When Sunday Silence was returned to Stone Farm from California after failing to sell at a two-year-old auction, the van that carried him crashed after the driver suffered a heart attack. The black colt dodged death once again.

Then, one year later, after a remarkable ascension under the skillful hands of trainer Charlie Whittingham,

Sunday Silence won the world's most famous race, the Kentucky Derby. But the racing world is full of doubters, many of whom were convinced Easy Goer, a colt he soundly defeated that day, was the better horse. Not until a late-season victory over that same rival in the championship-deciding Breeders' Cup Classic was Sunday Silence recognized as a true champion.

Yet the story doesn't end there. When injury cut short his racing career and Hancock brought him back to Stone Farm to stand as a stallion, indifference reared its ugly head again. Few people were interested in sending their mares to be bred to the horse, and Hancock accepted an offer to sell him to a leading Japanese breeder. In Japan, Sunday Silence became an immediate sensation, and ten years after leaving Kentucky, his sons and daughters are winning important races not only in Japan but throughout the world.

Sunday Silence was the ugly duckling, the horse nobody wanted, the overachiever, the fighter, all rolled into one. Perhaps, as Arthur Hancock suggested, he was a horse of destiny.

Ray Paulick
Lexington, Kentucky 2001

SUNDAY SILENCE

CHAPTER 1

Praying For A Miracle

In his younger days, if Arthur B. Hancock III was awake at three o'clock in the morning, it probably meant he was out carousing. But by 1986, Hancock, aged forty-three, was a family man. He and his wife, Staci, had recently moved their growing family into a beautiful new home on Stone Farm, a sprawling Thoroughbred nursery amidst the rolling hills of Bourbon County, Kentucky, in the heart of the Bluegrass.

Indeed, it was the very size of Stone Farm, all 3,800 acres of it, that was causing Hancock's sleepless nights. He was worried sick over how he was ever going to pay for the place.

Hancock, a fourth-generation horseman, moved to Stone Farm in 1970, at the request of his father, Arthur B. Hancock Jr., the legendary breeder known as "Bull."

The farm, just one hundred acres at the time, was adjacent to the mighty Claiborne Farm, which Bull Hancock had inherited when his father, the first Arthur B. Hancock, died in 1957. The third Arthur Hancock grew up on Claiborne, and he always expected that the farm started by his grandfather in 1910 would be his to run after his own father was gone.

When he moved to Stone Farm, Arthur thought it was similar to the time his grandfather sent Bull Hancock to run the family's original Thoroughbred farm, Ellerslie, near Charlottesville, Virginia. It was his chance, Arthur figured, to prepare himself for the day he would run Claiborne.

That day never came.

When Bull Hancock died at age sixty-two in 1972, his will did not choose either twenty-nine-year-old Arthur or his younger brother, Seth, then twenty-three, to run the farm. Instead, the executors and trustees of Hancock's estate were empowered to carry on Claiborne's business, with guidance from a three-man advisory committee. The committee consisted of Ogden Phipps, William Haggin Perry, and Charles Kenney, three close associates of Bull Hancock's.

At first, it appeared as if the two brothers would share in the management of Claiborne's day-to-day operations. "Seth and I have divided up the responsibility of the farm and its operation and we intend to carry on with the same high standards Dad set," Arthur Hancock told *Daily Racing Form*'s Joe Hirsch in November of 1972.

One month later, however, the three advisers were preparing to recommend Seth Hancock be named president of Claiborne, with Arthur relegated to a secondary role. Phipps, a longtime client of Claiborne and one of the most powerful men in racing, is said to have lobbied most heavily for the younger Hancock. Arthur got wind of their decision and during a meeting of the executors in December stood up and told them he was quitting. "Y'all run it like you want to," he said, according to a *Sports Illustrated* article. "You don't need me anymore. I'm out."

Hancock fled Claiborne with tears in his eyes and revenge on his mind. He hooked up with his lifelong friend, Paul Sullivan, and drowned himself in alcohol, something Hancock did with a fair amount of frequency in those days.

Drinking wasn't his only extracurricular activity. Hancock fancied himself as a musician, a poet, a philosopher, and a womanizer, not necessarily in that order. Introduced by his grandmother to the country music scene in Nashville as a young boy, Arthur graduated from the ukulele to the guitar, and by the time he was thirteen he was entertaining his friends with an impression of Elvis Presley, right down to the slicked-back, black-dyed hair and leather jacket. Bull Hancock found out about his son's singing appearance on a local radio station and stopped him in his tracks when Arthur returned later in the day to Claiborne.

"If it isn't the canary comin' home to roost," Bull said.

Those kind of comments hurt Arthur, but he didn't let them stop him from pursuing his interest in music. When it was time to go to college, Arthur chose Vanderbilt University, where he joined the swim team. Attending the Nashville school also gave him a chance to visit the Grand Ole Opry and dive deeper into the music scene.

Above all, though, Arthur was a horseman, a vocation that had coursed through the veins of Hancocks for more than a hundred years. His great-grandfather,

Captain Richard Johnson Hancock, was a Confederate soldier under Stonewall Jackson's command who had a gift for recognizing high-quality horseflesh. While Captain Hancock was nursing his Civil War wounds, hiding out from the Yankees in a wooded area of Virginia, he met and eventually wed Thomasia Overton Harris, whose family owned the massive Ellerslie estate. After the war Hancock began breeding Thoroughbreds at Ellerslie, and eventually acquired a stallion named Eolus, who soon developed a reputation as the top sire in the land.

Captain Hancock and his wife had four sons. One grew up to be a university professor and two became doctors. The fourth son, Arthur Boyd Hancock, born June 26, 1875, carried on the business of breeding Thoroughbreds, taking over from his father in 1909, three years before the elder Hancock's death, and becoming America's pre-eminent breeder.

From time to time the Hancocks had business in Kentucky, which is where Arthur Hancock met his future wife, Nancy Tucker Clay of Paris. Wed in 1908, the two inherited about 1,300 acres of land in Bourbon County. It was to become the foundation of Claiborne.

Arthur Hancock III, born February 22, 1943, remembers riding around Claiborne with his grandfather as a young boy, opening the gates for a few pennies a day, and checking on the mares and foals. Like his father, Arthur never seriously thought of doing anything in life other than breeding and raising horses.

In 1968, four years before his father's death, Arthur wrote a poem about the day he would be in charge:

"In the Back Yard"

One of the happiest times that I've had
Was in the back yard cooking steaks with my dad
The dogs lying by, and the sun going down
Fresh fallen leaves were all on the ground
Just us together, a boy and a man
Fixing our supper, a drink in our hand
He gazed out over the Bluegrass and said,
"This is yours someday, Arthur, after I'm dead
I've worked very hard for most all of my days
For you kids and your mother and son that's what pays
So you do your best, Bud, when you are the boss
Or all that I've worked for will quickly be lost."

...I may not succeed, Dad,

...But if ever you die

...I can promise you one thing,

...I'm going to try.

But running Claiborne wasn't to be.

His life on the family farm flashed before his eyes as Hancock ordered round after round of Budweisers that dark December day in 1972. He and Sullivan were hunkered down at Halls on the River, a restaurant and bar south of Paris, and the night was getting late.

Rather than feel sorry for his friend, Sullivan challenged Hancock. "You don't really want to do anything in life, do you Arthur?" Sullivan said. "All you want to do is drink and play that guitar!"

Hancock thought about his friend's comment for a minute, then said, "Sullivan, one of these days I'm going to win the Kentucky Derby and be bigger than Claiborne."

To which Sullivan responded, "Waitress, bring this fool another Budweiser."

Less than ten years later, however, Hancock made good on those promises.

The first two masters of Claiborne Farm achieved

prodigious success as Thoroughbred breeders. The first Arthur Hancock led North America's breeders nine times in races won and five times in money won. Bull Hancock was leading North American breeder by money won four times. The farm produced some of the industry's top stallions, including eight-time leading sire Bold Ruler, who was foaled at Claiborne. When they felt the breed needed an infusion of fresh blood, the Hancocks were not afraid to look elsewhere for stallions. Arthur Hancock imported Europeans Sir Gallahad III in 1924 and Blenheim II in 1936, and Bull brought Nasrullah to the farm from Ireland in 1951.

Despite all of the farm's success, however, a Claiborne-owned horse had never won the Kentucky Derby. Johnstown, bred by Arthur Hancock, won the 1939 Derby for Belair Stud, but twenty-six others, bred by Arthur or Bull Hancock, had run in the Derby, and all had failed. Bull Hancock's last chance to run for the roses came in 1969, when Dike carried Claiborne's orange colors to a third-place finish behind Majestic Prince.

"Daddy never did win the Derby, and he wanted to win it more than anything," Arthur said. "I always wished he had. That's the main reason I told Paul I wanted to win the race. I wanted to win it for Daddy. But I thought I might be seventy-five years old before I did it."

Hancock made his first run for Derby glory under the Twin Spires of Churchill Downs in 1981 with Tap Shoes, a colt he and New York businessman Leone J. Peters bred and owned in partnership. Tap Shoes had won Hialeah Park's Flamingo Stakes, an important prep race in Florida, but was scratched by trainer Horatio Luro from what was to be his final prep, the Blue Grass Stakes at Keeneland, when the track came up sloppy. Tap Shoes finished a well-beaten fourteenth behind Pleasant Colony in the Derby.

Later that summer, Gato Del Sol, a gray son of Stone Farm stallion Cougar II, won the Del Mar Futurity, an important race for two-year-olds in California, renewing the Derby dreams for the same partnership of Hancock and Peters. Trained by Eddie Gregson, Gato Del Sol came into the 1982 Derby as a 21-1 long shot, despite running a deceptively good second to Linkage in the Blue Grass Stakes.

Veteran jockey Eddie Delahoussaye, breaking Gato Del Sol from the number eighteen post position in a

nineteen-horse Derby field, allowed the colt to settle into last place for the opening half-mile, then steadily picked off horses one by one. Running on the outside part of the track, Gato Del Sol raced into tenth place with a half-mile left to run, and was fifth and gaining when the field turned into the long straightaway. Delahoussaye moved the colt to the front with only an eighth of a mile to go, and they bounded away to win by two and a half lengths.

The first part of Hancock's vow had been fulfilled.

"I felt I could walk on air," Hancock said of Gato Del Sol's Derby victory. "I'll never forget that when I moved in to Stone Farm, I sat on the back porch of the little house and thought about what I wanted to accomplish. I said to myself, more than anything else, what I want to do is win the Kentucky Derby. When it happened, it was like a fairy tale."

Claiborne did get its first Derby win two years later, when homebred Swale won the 1984 renewal.

By 1982 Stone Farm had grown in size from the hundred-acre plot of land leased from Claiborne to more than 2,600 acres. The late 1970s and early 1980s were a bustling time for the Thoroughbred industry.

Times were good for breeders, whose foals and year-lings were bringing record prices at auctions.

Arthur Hancock had grown some, too. A little over two years after his bitter departure from Claiborne, he met Staci Worthington, a Louisville girl who was work-ing at the horse sales in nearby Lexington for Warner Jones, who was the first consignor at Thoroughbred sales to hire women to show his horses. The concept was so unique, *Fortune* magazine ran an article with a photo of his female staff. They married in 1977. For the most part, the time and energy Arthur used to spend, in his words, as a "freewheelin', hard-drinkin', guitar-pickin', bar-brawlin', skirt-chasin' fool," now were focused on expanding Stone Farm and starting a family.

Hancock had purchased the original one-hundred acres from Claiborne and added adjacent parcels over the next several years, making it an 844-acre spread when he married Staci. That same year he added 1,500 more acres. His wife said he was obsessed with becom-ing bigger than Claiborne, working from dawn till dusk, clearing the land, putting up fences, and building barns.

The opportunity to make good on his second vow came shortly after Gato Del Sol's Derby. That fall, a 1,200-

acre farm owned by William du Pont became available and Hancock made an offer to buy it. Added to its existing 2,600 acres, the new property would give Stone Farm 3,800 acres, compared with Claiborne's 3,400.

"I'll never forget the Saturday morning when the Realtor called me and said, 'Guess what, Arthur? Bill is going to take your offer,' " Hancock recalled. "I thought I was going to have a stroke, because when I had made the offer I really didn't think he'd take it. I felt like my heart was going to jump out of my chest."

He remembered the old saying: Be careful what you wish for, you just might get it.

"My buying that farm was like a frog trying to eat a watermelon," he said later. "I already had a ton of debt and then I had to borrow more. But, I was at last bigger than Claiborne. I had fulfilled my greedy vow."

Despite his concerns over how he was going to pay for the new land, Hancock's chest puffed up with pride over his accomplishment. He said to Sam Ransom, a longtime farmhand who had left Claiborne to work for Arthur at Stone Farm, "Isn't it something, Sam? We're now bigger than Claiborne."

"Well," said Ransom, a great wit who often spoke in

rhymes, "we may be bigger in size, but Claiborne's big otherwise."

"That took the wind right out of my sails," Hancock said. "It floored me. I thought I was the Bourbon County land baron and suddenly realized that I was, but it was spelled 'B-A-R-R-E-N.' "

If Hancock was worried about how he was going to make his mortgage payments and pay all his bills in 1982, when the horse industry was going strong, the picture was far bleaker in 1986 when the economic bottom began falling out of the commercial market for Thoroughbreds. "I had yearly interest payments of almost a million and a half dollars," he said. "When the market dropped, everything we owned was worth thirty cents on the dollar."

Hancock asked his close friend Sullivan to look at his financial records and tell him what he could do.

"Hawk, you're gone," Sullivan said to Hancock, sadly. "There's no way you can possibly pull out of this, short of a miracle."

Hancock figured it was only a matter of time before he would have to file bankruptcy.

"There were many mornings that I would get up at

three o'clock and walk out on the farm and ask God to send me that miracle," he said.

On February 3, 1986, Staci Hancock gave birth to the couple's first son, who was named Arthur B. Hancock IV. It was a day of joy, not only for Arthur and Staci, but for all the Hancocks who had been hoping the couple would have a boy to carry on the family name. Arthur and Staci already had four girls, Walker, Hutchison, Kate, and Alex. A fifth daughter, Lynn, was born the following year.

Seven weeks after little Arthur was born there was another significant birth at Stone Farm, though no one knew how important it was at the time. Wishing Well, a mare by Understanding who had had difficulty with her previous pregnancies, gave birth on March 25, 1986, to a nearly jet-black colt sired by Halo.

It was Arthur Hancock's miracle. Sunday Silence had arrived.

CHAPTER 2

Providential

T om Tatham was one in a growing number of businessmen in the late 1970s and early 1980s who were attracted to Thoroughbred racing and breeding. As market prices soared, new investors rushed into the business to help fuel the increased demand for top-quality horseflesh. As a result the size of the North American Thoroughbred foal crop hit an all-time high in 1986, when 51,293 foals were registered with The Jockey Club, the breed's official registry. That was more than double the number registered only fifteen years earlier.

Tatham, a native Californian, had moved to Houston, Texas, to get in the oil business. He dabbled in Quarter Horses for several years before deciding in 1979, at the age of thirty-two, to take a serious plunge into Thoroughbred breeding. Tatham put together a partnership, Oak Cliff Thoroughbreds, with Texas horseman Ted Keefer, attorney Lukin Gilliland, and bloodstock agent John Adger. The latter was a longtime friend of Arthur Hancock, who introduced Tatham to Hancock during a trip to Kentucky.

With Tatham as managing partner of Oak Cliff, the partnership reached out through a network of people with money from the then-booming oil business and an interest in horses. They raised nearly six million dollars, which amounted to about half the amount of money Tatham himself had put up for the investment. The partnership made its first big splash in 1981 at the November breeding stock sale held at Keeneland in Lexington, spending some $3.7 million to be the sale's second-leading buyer. Oak Cliff's plan was to sell most of the female offspring that its new mares would produce but keep the colts and form new partnerships to race them.

The strategy worked well. By 1986 five colts from the original partnership had raced, and all five either won or placed in stakes races. Foremost among those runners was Skywalker, 10-1 upset winner of the three-million-dollar Breeders' Cup Classic in 1986. Michael Whittingham, the son of Charlie Whittingham, the Hall of Fame trainer who would later turn Sunday Silence into a champion, conditioned Skywalker.

Tatham hadn't expected the oil business to turn sour, but when it did in the mid-1980s, many of his Oak Cliff partners wanted out. He liquidated the original Oak Cliff Thoroughbreds partnership and formed a second business entity. Beginning in 1986, all of the foals bred by Oak Cliff would be offered at public auction. That was the year the Thoroughbred industry's commercial market began its rapid descent. It also was the year Sunday Silence was born.

Tatham had purchased Wishing Well privately in 1982 when the mare was in foal to Effervescing, an Ogden Phipps-bred turf specialist who had enjoyed only moderate success as a stallion. She delivered a healthy foal, but some time later it was found dead in a field, apparently struck by lightning. In 1983 Wishing Well was bred to 1976 Kentucky Derby winner Bold Forbes, one of eleven stallions Hancock was standing at Stone Farm at the time. Oak Cliff tried to sell Wishing Well that fall, but she failed to meet her reserve price and was brought back to Stone Farm. The mating to Bold Forbes failed when she aborted twins.

Meanwhile, Tatham had made another major financial commitment when, in February of 1984, he orchestrated the purchase of Halo, a top stallion who had been standing alongside the legendary Northern Dancer at Windfields Farm in Maryland. Windfields was owned by the Canadian industrialist E.P. Taylor.

Halo was red-hot, having sired the previous year's Kentucky Derby winner, Sunny's Halo, and North America's top two-year-old colt of 1983, Devil's Bag. The success of those two colts carried the son of Hail to Reason to the top of the leading general sire list by progeny earnings. When Halo turned fifteen years old in 1984, Windfields announced that his stud fee would more than triple, from $30,000 to $100,000, payable after a mare produced a live foal.

That's when Tatham stepped in, upping the ante considerably. He put together a syndicate of breeders willing to pay an astounding $900,000 per share, and purchased twenty-seven of the forty shares, giving him controlling interest in the stallion. The deal, struck when bloodstock values were spiraling upwardly at a dizzying pace, meant Halo was worth $36 million, at least in theory, since each of the forty shares was worth

$900,000. A revised stud fee was not announced by Tatham, who said the new shareholders planned either to breed their own mares to Halo or make arrangements with mare owners to foal share, a relatively common practice where the stallion shareholder and mare owner form a partnership and co-own the resulting foal from a mating. Based on the share price, however, the value of a stud fee was estimated to be $200,000.

Tatham opted to stand Halo at Stone Farm, and the stallion was quickly moved from Maryland to Kentucky in time for the beginning of the breeding season in mid-February. One of the mares bred to Halo that year was Wishing Well, but the mating failed to produce a pregnancy that lasted. Tatham tried again in 1985, and the result was Sunday Silence.

As a racehorse Halo was not a world-beater, though his combination of pedigree and racing performance was enough to make him a top stallion prospect. John R. Gaines, who developed the showplace operation Gainesway Farm on Paris Pike outside of Lexington purchased Halo's dam, the stakes-winning Cosmah. Cosmah's dam, Almahmoud, a daughter of Mahmoud, also produced Natalma, a filly sired by the once-beaten

champion Native Dancer. Natalma, in turn, produced Northern Dancer, the most influential sire in the modern era of Thoroughbred breeding.

Gaines paid a reported $75,000 in 1962 to purchase Cosmah, who already had produced the champion filly Tosmah for Gene Mori. A commercial breeder, Gaines sent all of Cosmah's subsequent foals to public auction, including her 1969 colt, Halo, who fetched $100,000 from Charles W. Engelhard at the 1970 Keeneland July yearling sale. Engelhard was a deep-pocketed buyer who, that summer, was enjoying a very successful run with the Northern Dancer colt Nijinsky II. A champion in England and Ireland at two and three years of age, Nijinsky II won England's Triple Crown in 1970, the first horse to do so since Bahram in 1935. Engelhard had purchased the colt in Canada as a yearling for a then-record $84,000, and he syndicated him to stand at Claiborne Farm for $5,440,000.

Engelhard died in 1971 before Halo raced, but his widow carried on the Cragwood Stables that he had made so successful. Trained by Mackenzie Miller, Halo raced just twice as a two-year-old, winning a maiden race at New York's Belmont Park in October. He began his three-year-old campaign with three consecutive victories, and then placed in several stakes races before Miller switched him from dirt to turf, where he won the mile and a quarter Lawrence Realization Stakes at Belmont Park in his third try on that surface. He managed to win a minor stakes race on dirt that fall, the Voters Handicap at a mile, at Laurel racetrack in Maryland.

Halo had less success as a four-year-old in 1973, placing in just one stakes race, and at the end of the year it was announced that he had been sold for $600,000 to Hollywood movie producer, Irving Allen, to stand at Allen's Derisley Wood Stud in Newmarket, England. However, the deal was rescinded when Allen learned that Halo was a cribber, a horse that liked to affix his teeth to things such as wood fences or stall doors and suck in air. It is a vice disdained by most horse owners because it can cause throat problems.

It turned out to be a fortuitous problem. Halo enjoyed his greatest racing success the following year as a five-year-old, first winning the Tidal Handicap at Aqueduct, after which he was sold to Windfields Farm. Following a narrow loss in the Bernard Baruch Handicap, Halo turned in his best performance, winning the United

Nations Handicap at Atlantic City Race Course in New Jersey. It was an important victory for a stallion prospect, since the United Nations was accorded grade I status by the Thoroughbred Owners and Breeders Association, which, as an aid to breeders or auction buyers, ranks the best North American races as either grade I, grade II, or grade III. Halo was to race in the Marlboro Cup, a grade I dirt race at Belmont Park that fall, but an injury forced him into retirement. Windfields syndicated Halo into forty shares at $30,000 apiece.

Halo's sire, Hail to Reason, was a son of Turn-to, an Irish-bred son of Royal Charger, who was brought to America as a yearling and raced for Captain Harry Guggenheim, a client of Bull Hancock's Claiborne Farm. Turn-to was a top two-year-old and was the springtime favorite for the 1954 Kentucky Derby, when a bowed tendon abruptly ended his racing career. Turn-to sired twenty-five stakes winners, but his major contribution to the breed is as a sire of sires. His sons at stud included Sir Gaylord, Best Turn, Cyane, First Landing, and Hail to Reason, all of whom have been represented by additional sons or grandsons at stud. Hail to Reason is the most important of Turn-to's stallion sons. In addition to siring Halo, who has numerous sons and grandsons at stud, he is the sire of Roberto, a champion for the Galbreath family's Darby Dan Farm, who has begun his own branch of the sire line descending from Royal Charger.

The female side of Sunday Silence's pedigree is not as distinguished. Wishing Well, who developed into a top-class stakes performer for West Coast trainer Gary Jones, was sired by Understanding, a California stallion who had just one other stakes winner during his career at stud. Understanding did have one thing in common with Hail to Reason, the grandsire on the top of Sunday Silence's pedigree. Both horses were bred and raced by the Bieber-Jacobs Stable of Hall of Fame trainer Hirsch Jacobs and his partner, Isidore Bieber. Hail to Reason was the champion two-year-old of 1960, when he won nine of eighteen starts before suffering a career-ending injury. Understanding, a son of Promised Land, was produced from Pretty Ways, a daughter of the fabled Stymie, who in the 1940s rose from the bottom claiming ranks to earn almost a million dollars. Understanding raced over five years, winning seven of eighty-seven starts. He won a solo stakes race, the

Stuyvesant Handicap under a feathery 110 pounds at Aqueduct in 1966. Understanding placed in six other stakes races before his career ended.

Wishing Well was bred by George A. Pope Jr., a California lumber and steamship magnate who owned the El Peco Ranch in the Golden State's San Joaquin Valley. Active in racing and breeding for most of his life, Pope won the 1962 Kentucky Derby with his homebred colt Decidedly, a son of 1954 Derby winner Determine. Pope also bred and owned J.O. Tobin, a champion in England and co-champion sprinter of 1978 in North America. J.O. Tobin is best remembered as the horse that ended Triple Crown winner Seattle Slew's perfect record with an upset in the 1977 Swaps Stakes at Hollywood Park.

Pope's imprint is all over the female side of Wishing Well's pedigree. Her dam, Mountain Flower, a non-winner of seven starts, was sired by Montparnesse II, an Argentine-bred horse who raced in Pope's colors in his native country before being sent north to race in America and stand at El Peco Ranch. Wishing Well's second dam, Edelweiss, also bred by Pope, was sired by the El Peco Ranch stallion Hillary, bred and raced by

Pope in the 1950s. Hillary, a son of Khaled, sired Hill Rise, who finished second for Pope in the 1964 Kentucky Derby behind Northern Dancer.

Breeders with large drafts of horses often are forced to make tough decisions, and Pope elected to run Wishing Well in claiming races during her three-year-old season in 1978 and at four the following year. There were no takers at the claiming box when the filly won a maiden claiming race in September of her three-year-old campaign or in her next start, when she carried a claiming price of $20,000. Wishing Well had begun her career in Northern California, but in the spring of the following year, with just two victories from ten starts, she was sent to the Southern California barn of trainer Tommy Doyle.

Entered for the first time at Hollywood Park with a claiming price of $25,000 and sent off at odds of 21-1, Wishing Well raced on the lead and set very fast fractions in a seven-furlong dirt race, but lost in the final jump. That effort captured the attention of Jeff Siegel, a denizen of the press box who developed his own speed figures, handicapped the races for several newspapers, and also owned some horses that were

trained by Gary Jones.

Jones was on the lookout for a horse to claim for Mike Lima, a former owner who had been out of the business for about ten years. Siegel said Wishing Well was the horse.

"He said if I didn't claim this filly next time she ran he'd never help me claim another one," Jones remembered. When Wishing Well was entered again, this time carrying a $32,000 claiming price, Jones followed Siegel's advice. The June 2 race, at eight and a half furlongs, was run on the turf, marking the first time Wishing Well had tried that surface. She came from just off the pace and won going away, by nine widening lengths in the stretch. Wishing Well had found a new home and a new barn.

Jones and Lima ran Wishing Well back in an allowance race three weeks later, and she won again, this time by three and a half lengths. She was jumped into stakes competition next in the Convenience Stakes and won again, this time by a length.

"When I first got her she was loco," Jones said of Wishing Well. "We spent a lot of time with her, and Jorge Ochoa, her exercise rider, really got her to settle."

Jones picked jockey Fernando Toro, a turf specialist, as her regular rider.

Wishing Well won two more races that year, including the Autumn Days Handicap at the Oak Tree meeting at Santa Anita, but it was not until the following summer at Hollywood Park that the five-year-old mare blossomed. It was also at Hollywood Park where she and another five-year-old mare, Country Queen, developed a brief but memorable rivalry.

The two met ten times over a two-year period, with Wishing Well holding the edge by a six-to-four margin, but their rivalry reached its peak over a two-month period at Hollywood Park in the summer of 1980.

The Gamely Handicap, a grade II event, was run on May 4, one day after Genuine Risk had defeated the California-bred Rumbo to win the Kentucky Derby. Hollywood Park introduced two innovations that meeting designed to bring out more fans. The first, pick six wagering, caught on quickly, with bettors hoping to hit a jackpot by picking the winners of six consecutive races. The wager was modeled after a similar bet offered for years at Agua Caliente in Tijuana, Mexico. When no one picked all six winners, the money was

carried over to the next racing program. The other new wrinkle was a gift giveaway program Hollywood Park was trying for the first time.

On May 4, the combination of pick six wagering and a tote bag giveaway attracted an all-time record crowd of 80,348 fans to Hollywood Park. They witnessed some pretty good racing, including an exciting come-from-behind victory by Wishing Well, who collared Country Queen in the final furlong and won the nine-furlong Gamely by a length. Country Queen carried 123 pounds as the high weight of the race. Wishing Well was assigned 119.

Seventeen days later Country Queen got Wishing Well's measure, winning the mile and a sixteenth Hawthorne Handicap by a length and a half, this time with only a one-pound difference in the weights, 122 for Country Queen to 121 for Wishing Well. Next time out, in the Wilshire Handicap, the same distance as the Hawthorne, Country Queen was packed with 124 pounds, with Wishing Well at 120. The two were at identical odds in their first two meetings, but in the Wilshire, Country Queen was made the heavy favorite, at 7-5, while Wishing Well was 3-1. Country Queen made the lead turning for home, but Toro and his filly ran her down from the outside to win. A crowd of 49,250 turned out for the race, lured in part by another Hollywood Park giveaway.

Their final Hollywood Park meeting came two weeks later, in the Beverly Hills Handicap. The racing secretary weighted the two mares at an identical 122 pounds. Bettors favored Country Queen slightly and made her the 2-1 favorite. At the end of the nine furlongs, the two mares were almost inseparable. Country Queen came from just off the pace, then opened up a length and a half advantage inside the eighth pole. Toro had Wishing Well in full flight. She gained steadily as the finish approached, but Country Queen held on to win by a nose.

The two met once more, at Del Mar racetrack just north of San Diego, in the one-mile Palomar Handicap. Country Queen again carried high weight, 123 pounds, while Wishing Well was assigned 121. Wishing Well lost another tough one, getting nosed out at the finish, this time by a new shooter named A Thousand Stars. Country Queen ran fourth.

The Wishing Well-Country Queen rivalry captured

the interest of Southern California racing fans during that summer of 1980, but it would be nothing like the rivalry her son created with Easy Goer later that decade.

"She was one of the career beginners for me," said Jones, who went on to train a number of outstanding runners, including Turkoman, the champion older horse of 1986 and second to Skywalker in that year's Breeders' Cup Classic. "Old Wishing Well always laid her body down for us. She was game."

Tatham agreed. "She was very tenacious, a trait you like to pass on," he said.

Wishing Well won one more race as a six-year-old in 1981, then was retired with twelve wins from thirty-eight starts and earnings of $381,625. Her pedigree and race record attracted the attention of Tom Tatham, who purchased her the following year.

But her greater glory was yet to come.

CHAPTER 3

A Tough Sell

T he mating of Wishing Well to Halo was chosen by Tom Tatham because it would create an inbreeding to Mahmoud, the Epsom Derby winner of 1936 owned and bred by the Aga Khan. Mahmoud was a son of Blenheim II, the British sire imported to Claiborne Farm by Arthur Hancock prior to the 1937 breeding season. Mahmoud, also imported to stand in Kentucky at Cornelius Vanderbilt Whitney's farm, is the sire of Almahmoud, the second dam of Halo. The second strain of Mahmoud in Sunday Silence's pedigree is found with him as the sire of Mahmoudess, the dam of Promised Land, sire of Wishing Well's sire, Understanding.

Devil's Bag is also inbred to Mahmoud, and Tatham had found several other instances of that particular pedigree pattern that produced superior runners.

Tatham also discovered, much to his dismay, that Halo's offspring had some physical traits that turned off yearling buyers. "His yearlings weren't the most physically attractive ones at the sale," Tatham said. "He has certain traits show up that are less aesthetic. He got a lot of horses that had a 'Roman nose,' and a fair number that are back at the knee." Back at the knee means simply that the front legs, instead of being vertically straight, are bent slightly back at the knee joint.

Yearlings from Halo's first crop sold for an average price of just $44,625 in 1980, but in 1984, the year he was moved to Stone Farm, his yearling average reached $158,885. Yearlings from his first Kentucky crop of foals averaged $180,333, but by the time Sunday Silence sold in 1987, the stallion's yearling average had slipped to $109,944. That wasn't the kind of number Tatham had in mind when he paid $900,000 per share for the stallion.

Astute horsemen such as Arthur Hancock sometimes can sense when a young foal is going to turn into something special as a racehorse. There's something about the way it carries itself, the domineering personality it shows when put into a paddock with other young horses after they are weaned. Sunday Silence, who was raised on a section of Stone Farm called Walnut Lea, was not that kind of horse. According to Hancock, the only thing that made him stand out was his backward appearance.

But the history of the turf is filled with great horses that overcame crooked legs or unsightly appearances to run like the wind. More than a few of those bad-legged or bad-looking horses were raised at Claiborne. "I remember my Daddy laughing about how he once told one of the men to take this mare, Miss Disco, and her foal and put them on the back of the farm because the foal was so ugly. Well, of course, that foal was Bold Ruler."

Bold Ruler, a son of Nasrullah, was Horse of the Year in 1957 for Mrs. Henry Carnegie Phipps, the mother of Ogden Phipps. Bold Ruler had a record-setting run as a sire at Claiborne Farm, where he topped the sire list by progeny earnings for seven consecutive years, from 1963 until 1969, the longest such streak in North American history. He added an eighth sire title in 1973, the year his most famous offspring, Secretariat, swept the Triple Crown.

Those kinds of results on the racetrack and in the

breeding shed improve the appearance of any horse.

Hancock thought of his father and Bold Ruler whenever one of Tatham's advisers, Ted Keefer, came to Stone Farm to visit the Oak Cliff foals. "Ted would come in," Hancock said, "and when he'd see Sunday Silence — this was before he was named — he'd say, 'Put that black bastard away. God, that's an awful weanling.'

"The next time Ted would come to the farm he'd say, 'I don't even want to see that Wishing Well colt.' I would say to him that he'd improved, but he insisted. 'Oh, no, I don't want to even look at him. Put him back.' It was every time, almost like something out of the *Twilight Zone*. Eerie. We'd get to Barn One out at Walnut Lea and I didn't even have to say anything. Ted would shake his head and say, 'I don't want to see him.' It's like he hated the horse, and there really wasn't any reason to hate him."

During one visit when Keefer disparaged the colt, Hancock's farm manager, Pete Logan, reminded him that good horses, sometimes even Kentucky Derby winners, come in all types of packages. "Well, Mr. Keefer, roses will look mighty pretty on him one day.

You never know." Keefer shot back, "The only time that son of a bitch will ever have a rose on him will be on his grave."

Keefer wasn't the only one who didn't like what he saw when visiting Sunday Silence at the farm. Gary Jones, in addition to training Wishing Well, had some horses for Oak Cliff and was asked by Tatham to look at the foals during a visit to Kentucky. "I had a chance to train Sunday Silence," Jones said, "but his legs were so crooked they looked like coat hangers. Still, I said I'd like to see the colt in another six months to see how he looked then, but Keefer said, 'Gary, I want this foal and mare gone.' Ted was sending me some good horses from some other people in Texas, the Preston brothers and Mike Rutherford, and I couldn't go against him."

Tatham had several other trainers look at Sunday Silence before the Keeneland July sale in 1987, including Michael Whittingham, John Gosden, Eddie Gregson, and France's Maurice Zilbert. "I don't think anybody was keen at his prospects as a racehorse at that time," Tatham said.

Aside from the Thanksgiving incidence of diarrhea that nearly killed him, Sunday Silence had a fairly

uneventful upbringing. The colt was always difficult to handle, owing partly to the hot-blooded streak of his sire, Halo, who wore a muzzle to keep him from attacking the stallion grooms or visitors to the farm. He almost killed one groom, Hancock said.

"One time Halo reached down and bit a groom right in the stomach, had him down on the ground, and got down on his knees to try to finish the job," he recalled. "He was never a problem in the breeding shed, though. He always wanted to breed the mare."

Sunday Silence wasn't mean like his sire, but a rough-houser. Horses brought up at Stone Farm — whose longtime motto has been, "We're trying to raise you a good horse" — are "raised like rough boys from the mountains," Hancock told *The Blood-Horse* in 1988. "They develop good muscles and tendons rather than being dainty."

The expansiveness of the Stone Farm property gave young horses pastures of up to a hundred acres in which to run free. Hancock believed that wide-open spaces encouraged foals, weanlings, and yearlings to build muscle, strengthen bone, and develop into top athletes. The land he selected for the farm's growth was an important ingredient. Tall trees that withstood the "storms of time," he said, were an indication to him that the root systems go deep into the ground, meaning the soil is deep and full of minerals.

Sunday Silence wasn't accepted into the select sessions of Keeneland's July sale, which traditionally are held on a Monday and Tuesday. Instead, he was catalogued into a non-select session on the following day, Wednesday, July 22. For a yearling to gain entry into the select sessions, it must possess both a first-class pedigree and pass a physical inspection made by Keeneland officials. Obviously, Sunday Silence wouldn't impress an inspection team.

For many years the selected sessions of the Keeneland July sale had been the world's finest auction for Thoroughbred yearlings. It was at Keeneland that Halo sold as a yearling for $100,000 in 1970. The same sale set an all-time record when a son of Nijinsky II brought the unbelievable hammer price of $13.1 million in 1985, just two years before Sunday Silence was offered.

But bloodstock prices went into a free fall in the second half of the 1980s and dramatically affected the Keeneland July sale. The average price during the

select session reached $601,467 in 1984, more than tripling in just five years. More than thirty-three yearlings sold for a million dollars or more in the 1984 sale. Even with the record-priced $13.1-million yearling sold in 1985, the average at the Keeneland July sale declined to $537,129. By 1987 it fell to $372,736.

A daughter of Halo sold for $1,025,000 in 1986 at Fasig-Tipton's yearling sale in Saratoga Springs, New York, the year before Sunday Silence was to sell. The filly, named Lustre, who would go on to place in a stakes race, was the only offspring by Halo to reach the seven-figure mark at a yearling sale. Hancock and Tatham had no such hopes for the Halo colt out of Wishing Well when he walked into the sale ring on July 22, wearing a sticker on his hip representing number 454 in the Keeneland catalogue.

Tatham had left the sale to go to a son's graduation ceremony in Nashville, Tennessee, and Hancock bid on the colt when it became obvious that no one else wanted him. He signed the ticket as a buy-back for $17,000. "He would have only sold for ten thousand if I hadn't bid on him," Hancock said.

The 140 yearlings that sold during the July 22 session at Keeneland averaged $143,614, more than eight times higher than the number on the bid board when Sunday Silence was led out of the ring. In fact, only three yearlings sold for less that day.

Later, Hancock told Tatham he bought the colt back for him. "He went too cheap," Hancock said. "But Tom said to me he didn't want him, because Keefer didn't like him."

Hancock didn't argue the point. "I said that's okay, then thought to myself, 'I just blew another seventeen thousand dollars.' "

Sunday Silence was not the only Halo offspring that sold for less than Hancock and the Oak Cliff partners had hoped for. Hancock's friend Paul Sullivan was listed as the buyer for a Halo filly that stalled in the bidding at $25,000.

After the Keeneland debacle, Hancock asked Sullivan to buy a half-interest in Sunday Silence and they would try to sell him again the next year at a two-year-olds in training sale, along with the Halo filly later named Heavenly Call. Hancock sent the pair to Albert Yank, a veteran bloodstock agent in California, who entered them in a sale operated by the California Thoroughbred

Breeders Association and held at Hollywood Park in March. Hancock and Sullivan put a reserve price of $50,000 for the colt, and they ended up buying him back in the name of World Wide Bloodstock when bidding stalled at $32,000. Heavenly Call was bought back for $22,000. Immediately after the sale, Hancock thought Yank had found someone to buy both horses for $100,000, but that deal fell through.

"It almost seemed like destiny," Hancock said.

While in California for the sale, Hancock did convince Charlie Whittingham to buy a half-interest in both Sunday Silence and Heavenly Call. Whittingham paid $50,000 for his share in the two horses after Sullivan told Hancock he wanted out. "Hawk, if I stay in he'll probably break down," Sullivan said to Hancock of Sunday Silence, "and if I get out he'll probably win the Kentucky Derby."

Actually, Whittingham's purchase was not a cash deal but a trade of $50,000 in training fees in exchange for the two horses. He got his share in Sunday Silence without having to open his checkbook.

Midway on the long haul back from California to Kentucky, the driver of the horse van carrying

Hancock's horses suffered a heart attack in the Texas panhandle. The van careened off the road and tipped over. Sunday Silence suffered cuts and bruises and was treated at an Oklahoma veterinary clinic before being returned to Kentucky two weeks later.

"When he got back to the farm, our veterinarian said he thought the horse was a wobbler," Hancock said of Sunday Silence. Wobbler syndrome, usually caused by spinal cord compression, makes a horse uncoordinated and relatively useless as far as racing is concerned. "We decided to just turn him out in a paddock for a couple of weeks and he seemed to work out of that. Once again, I got very lucky."

A few weeks later, when Whittingham came to the Kentucky Derby with another Halo colt, Lively One, he and exercise rider Pam Mabes visited Hancock at Stone Farm and got a closer look at Sunday Silence and some of the farm's yearlings. It wasn't a pretty sight when the colt was led away from them, his hocks almost touching as he walked. "Oh, Charlie, look at that colt," Mabes said to Whittingham. "Look at those back legs."

It was then that Whittingham decided to hedge on

his investment, selling half of his share in Sunday Silence and Heavenly Call to Dr. Ernest Gaillard, a friend of the trainer who had previously owned horses with him. Whittingham, who could trade horses with the best of them, got his $50,000 investment back, and Hancock had a new partner.

Hancock's fortunes began to turn in 1988, even though he was unsuccessful in his efforts to sell Sunday Silence at the two-year-old sale in California. Late in the year, with the help of John Adger, Hancock purchased for an undisclosed price a two-year-old Halo filly named Goodbye Halo, after she had won the Demoiselle Stakes at Aqueduct for Texan John Ballis. Turned over to Whittingham, she romped to victory a few weeks later in the Hollywood Starlet, a $500,000 race at Hollywood Park that earned Hancock a quick $274,505 on his investment. The following winter, after Goodbye Halo defeated a strapping roan named Winning Colors in the Las Virgenes Stakes at Santa Anita, Hancock sold an interest in the filly to Lexington businessman Alex Campbell.

Goodbye Halo then finished third behind Winning Colors in the Santa Anita Oaks. Trainer D. Wayne

Lukas took a big chance and ran Winning Colors against colts in the Kentucky Derby, where she scored a front-running victory over Forty Niner, while Whittingham ran Goodbye Halo the previous day in the Kentucky Oaks. She defeated another Whittingham filly, Jeanne Jones, by daylight, giving Hancock an Oaks trophy to go with the Derby trophy he'd won with Gato Del Sol.

Hancock dedicated the 1982 Derby win to his late father, and the Oaks victory was dedicated to his mother, Waddell. "My Dad taught me what I know, and my mother kept him from drilling it into me too hard," *The Blood-Horse* quoted Hancock as saying.

Goodbye Halo went on to win the Mother Goose Stakes and Coaching Club American Oaks, both at Belmont Park, and then ran a determined third against Personal Ensign and Winning Colors in one of the most memorable Breeders' Cup races ever run, the 1988 Distaff at Churchill Downs. Goodbye Halo was beaten only a half-length for the win after a thrilling stretch run that saw the Ogden Phipps homebred, Personal Ensign, finish her career with a perfect thirteen-for-thirteen lifetime record. When Goodbye Halo retired

after the 1989 season, she had won eleven of twenty-four starts, including seven grade I races, and earned $1,706,702. Campbell and Hancock entered her as a broodmare prospect in January 1990 at Keeneland, and she sold for $2.1 million.

Hancock also gained additional glory, if not a financial reward, during the 1988 Triple Crown when Risen Star, a Secretariat colt he'd bred in partnership with Leone Peters, won the Preakness Stakes and then steamrolled the opposition in the Belmont, winning by fourteen and three-quarters lengths.

By this time, the name Sunday Silence officially had been registered with The Jockey Club for the 1986 foal by Halo out of Wishing Well. The name was suggested to Hancock by the Straw family of Ellicott City, Maryland, which, while discussing the 1987 Kentucky Derby over the dinner table, fantasized about what name they would give to a horse if the family had one run in the Derby. Phil and Becky Straw, along with daughters Amy and Emily, were not horse owners, though Phil Straw had attended the University of Kentucky and worked for a time at a Standardbred farm near Lexington.

The Straws discussed horse names in great detail and came up with a five-page typewritten list. One of the names on their list was Sunday Silence.

The family sent its list to three Kentucky farms, all of which responded with a note thanking them for the suggestions. "We liked Sunday Silence because of its alliteration and also because Sunday is a quiet day," Phil Straw said. Hancock also liked the name, in part because it reminded him of the Kris Kristofferson song "Sunday Morning Coming Down," which dealt with the hangovers that often ensued after a Saturday night of revelry.

Hancock could relate to those Sunday mornings, though in recent years he had slowed down his drinking and eventually quit altogether. On a flight back from California on Campbell's private jet after one of Goodbye Halo's big wins in 1987, Hancock was ready to celebrate the victory with a glass of wine. "What do you need that for?" Campbell said. "How could you possibly get a better high than the one we just had at the racetrack when that filly won?"

"You know, you're right," Hancock said. And with that, he decided to give up the bottle for good.

But the highs that Hancock got from Goodbye Halo were small compared with what was just around the corner with Sunday Silence.

CHAPTER 4

"Sunday Stop It"

A rthur Hancock knew Charlie Whittingham doled out praise in small doses, so he was surprised by what the Hall of Fame trainer had to say over the telephone one autumn morning in 1988. "Arthur," Whittingham said, "this black son of a bitch can run."

"Who's that?" Hancock asked.

"The one out of Wishing Well," the trainer replied.

Hancock flashed back to earlier in the year when he saw Sunday Silence gallop just before the two-year-olds in training sale at Hollywood Park, and to the previous year when the colt's appearance so repulsed Ted Keefer that he didn't even want to see him. Hancock, the black-sheep son of Bull Hancock who was rejected as the heir apparent to run Claiborne Farm, was beginning to like the Halo colt that had roused no interest. Whittingham's positive assessment of Sunday Silence's ability was music to his ears.

"I'm not saying I knew something about this horse or really liked him," Hancock would say later, "but I liked the way he moved at the two-year-old sale, and I stuck with him earlier because of the adviser who hated him so much."

Sunday Silence had been in Whittingham's barn for a couple of months, first at the San Luis Rey training center south of Los Angeles and later with his string at Santa Anita Park in the east Los Angeles suburb of Arcadia.

When the colt arrived at Santa Anita, Whittingham put his number one exercise rider, Janet Johnson, in charge of Sunday Silence's early-morning gallops. Johnson had galloped Whittingham's 1986 Kentucky Derby winner, Ferdinand, who was known as a lazy horse in the mornings, and she also had handled the champion turf mare Estrapade, among others.

But on his very first trip to the track under her, Sunday Silence was wild and unruly, and Johnson wanted no part of him. She brought the fiery colt back to the barn, jumped off, and said, "I don't want to get on that horse again."

Whittingham turned instead to Pam Mabes, another in a string of top-notch, bright-eyed horsewomen, known in some circles as "Charlie's Angels," who galloped and worked many of the trainer's best horses. Mabes recalled her visit to Stone Farm that spring when she first laid eyes on Sunday Silence. She didn't hold out a great deal of hope the colt was going to turn into anything special.

Whittingham had built his Hall of Fame career on getting the most out of every horse that passed through his hands. Born in 1913 near San Diego, California, Charlie Whittingham followed his older brother, Joe, to the racetrack in Tijuana, Mexico, and first worked as a hot walker and groom. Joe started out as a jockey, but soon became too big for the occupation and turned to training. A few years later, Charlie went to the racetrack, too, training a few cheap horses while also working as a jockey's agent. He hit all the California tracks doing both, including Santa Anita Park's opening day on Christmas of 1934.

In the early 1940s, Whittingham went to work as assistant trainer to Horatio Luro, the debonair South American horseman who attracted high-society owners such as Liz Tippett of Llangollen Farm. The two men made quite a team, winning a number of big races, but it

wasn't long before Whittingham heard another calling, this one from the U.S. Marines, shortly after the Japanese bombed Pearl Harbor in December of 1941.

Whittingham was assigned to the Pacific theater, patrolling the Solomon Islands, an area east of New Guinea that was in the reach of Japanese troops and was the scene of one of the war's most famous battles, Guadalcanal.

Whittingham avoided injury but contracted malaria, a disease doctors suspect caused the trainer's hair to fall out prematurely, leading to his well-known nickname, the Bald Eagle. Whittingham didn't see action during the remainder of the war. He returned to the mainland in the spring of 1944, when he met a North Carolina girl named Peggy Boone. They were married later that year, and soon thereafter Whittingham was reunited with Luro on the East Coast. He then went back to California with a string of Luro's horses in 1947. The next year Whittingham went out on his own, remembering Luro's admonition to "never squeeze the lemon dry" when it came to his horses.

For the next four decades, Whittingham won just about every major race in California and made numerous successful excursions to the East. He trained his first champion, Porterhouse, the top two-year-old male of 1953. Eighteen years and more than 125 stakes wins later Whittingham guided Ack Ack through a Horse of the Year campaign and also won the first of his three Eclipse Awards as outstanding trainer.

While Llangollen Farm supplied most of Whittingham's best horses early in his career, the Bald Eagle's client list expanded to a "Who's Who" of Thoroughbred racing and breeding. One of those clients was Bull Hancock, who in 1966 imported a South American champion named Forli, syndicated him for $960,000, and turned him over to Whittingham to train.

As he did with many foreign horses, Whittingham took his time with Forli, not racing the colt until mid-way through the following year. The chestnut son of Aristophanes won his first two American starts easily, then suffered a career-ending injury while finishing second in the Citation Handicap at Arlington Park. When it was time to take Forli to Claiborne Farm, where the following year he began a long career at stud, Bull Hancock's two sons, Arthur and Seth, were

assigned vanning duties. It was the first time that Arthur met Whittingham, though he recalled from his childhood seeing the trainer with jockey Bill Shoemaker playing croquet on the lawn at Claiborne Farm. Whittingham and Arthur Hancock took an immediate liking to one another, though it would be nearly twenty years later before Whittingham would have any major success with one of Hancock's horses, Infinidad, a multiple stakes winner in 1986 and 1987. Then came Goodbye Halo in late 1987 and 1988.

Sunday Silence would take the collaboration between Whittingham and Hancock to another level of success.

One of the people most responsible for Sunday Silence's success was Pam Mabes, who grew up in San Pedro, a harbor town south of Los Angeles, and joined the Whittingham stable just prior to the 1987 Breeders' Cup. One of the horses Whittingham assigned her to gallop was Lively One, another talented but temperamental son of Halo. She accompanied the colt to Churchill Downs for the 1988 Kentucky Derby, where Lively One, an 18-1 long shot, finished a well-beaten twelfth behind the filly Winning Colors.

When Sunday Silence came along, Mabes could see immediately he was going to be a real challenge. "He had no discipline," she said. "Charlie wanted me to take him to the track and walk to the eighth pole, then jog to the wire. But there was no way he'd do that. He'd want to take off, buck, jump, or do anything except what I wanted him to do. People around the track were asking why Charlie would let that girl get on that horse, that she couldn't control him."

As always, though, Whittingham knew what he was doing with the horse. He sent Mabes and Sunday Silence out with the first set each morning, before the track was open for training. Sunday Silence had to cool his heels by the track's entrance, waiting for the gates to open. He learned patience, at least a measure of it.

"He'd behave himself for a few minutes; then the next thing he was rearing, leaping, and jumping," she said.

"But that was Charlie's thing. Let him act up, run off, whatever. He didn't want us to fight the horses; he wanted them to be happy. He knew each day they'd run off a little bit less. Charlie had so much patience."

Getting Sunday Silence into a galloping mode each

morning was just part of the problem. His style of galloping made it tough for Mabes to stay on board. "He'd get to about the quarter pole, then put his head down between his legs and start to buck as hard as he could. I thought I'd tumble right over the front of him. It's amazing I never came off him."

The colt's antics prompted his exercise rider to give Sunday Silence a nickname. "He'd go into his little routine and I'd start saying 'Sunday Stop It.' " The name stuck.

Mabes and "Sunday Stop It" became a source of entertainment for some. Willard Proctor, a contemporary of Whittingham's who also trained his first set of horses as soon as the track opened, used to watch with amusement as Mabes struggled with Sunday Silence each morning. "He'd sit at the same place every day, around the three-eighths pole, and when I galloped past he'd have himself a good laugh," Mabes said.

One day, as Sunday Silence neared his first race, Whittingham asked Bill Shoemaker to stop by the barn and give the colt a workout to see what he thought of him. Shoemaker, who was fifty-four years old when he won the Derby with Ferdinand in 1986, was happy to oblige, but it was on a day when Sunday Silence wasn't on his best behavior.

Mabes watched from the grandstand to see how the Hall of Fame rider would handle the unruly colt. "Shoe took him to the training track first to warm him up a little," she said. "No pony, his irons jacked up pretty high. I was amazed. Sunday was up to all his antics."

Shoemaker worked Sunday Silence and then rushed the colt back to the barn and jumped off. "Don't ever put me on that crazy son of a bitch again," he said to Whittingham. "Send him back to a farm and get him broke!"

"Getting a little old and scared?" Whittingham chided.

By this time, though, Whittingham knew he had a colt with talent. One morning Whittingham worked him in company with another horse from his stable, and Mabes was doing everything she could to keep him throttled down and running alongside his workmate. "I had this feeling that if I gave him just a little rein he'd open up ten lengths on the other horse," Mabes said. She brought Sunday Silence back to the barn with a big smile on her face. Whittingham returned the smile with a wink, and then said, "I think

we got us a good one, girl."

With Shoemaker, his number one jockey, out of the picture, Whittingham turned to another rider, Patrick Valenzuela, a gifted athlete whose career was sidetracked on numerous occasions because of drugs. "Patrick really got along with the horse," Mabes recalled.

So did Aaron Gryder, an eighteen-year-old apprentice rider who exercised a number of Whittingham horses in the mornings. Gryder was aboard Sunday Silence for his first recorded workout at Santa Anita. "He was definitely a project," Gryder said, "but you also knew he was a quality horse. I could tell that the first time I rode him. He worked in company that day with another horse, going five furlongs in 1:02 4/5."

Whittingham entered Sunday Silence in a six and a half-furlong maiden race during the Oak Tree Racing Association meeting at Santa Anita on October 30. Hancock and Whittingham, however, had more of their attention focused on Louisville, Kentucky, where Goodbye Halo was gearing up for the Breeders' Cup Distaff, to be run at Churchill Downs one week later. (It turned out to be the race of the year, with Ogden Phipps'

Personal Ensign getting up in the final stride for a miraculous come-from-behind victory over the front-running Winning Colors. Goodbye Halo was gallant in defeat, finishing only a half-length behind at the wire.)

Many horseplayers interpreted Whittingham's patient nature to mean that his first-time starters would usually need to run at least one race before they were ready to win. Nevertheless, Sunday Silence attracted enough attention in his morning workouts to be bet down to 3-2 as the favorite in his career debut. As it turned out, Sunday Silence was no different than many of Whittingham's other first-time starters: he did need a race under his girth.

Breaking from the number eleven post in a twelve-horse field of two-year-olds, Sunday Silence left the gate a step slowly, but Valenzuela quickly put him in contention before a quarter-mile had been run. He raced head and head for the lead around the turn, opened up a one-length advantage after five furlongs, then was overtaken in the final hundred yards, losing by a neck to Caro Lover. The *Daily Racing Form* chart caller noted that Sunday Silence "raced greenly."

Two weeks later, on November 13, Sunday Silence

was entered in another maiden race for two-year-olds, this one at six furlongs at Hollywood Park in Inglewood, California. The fans, obviously not put off by the colt's losing performance in his first race, made him the odds-on favorite at 7-10 in a field of ten. He ran like a heavy favorite should, stalking the early leader, taking command before entering the stretch, and drawing off to win by ten lengths in a very fast time for the six furlongs, 1:09 2/5.

Remembering the motto of his mentor, Whittingham decided not to squeeze the lemon too dry. He entered Sunday Silence just once more in 1988, an allowance race at Hollywood Park going six and a half furlongs. Sunday Silence faced six others, including Houston, a son of Triple Crown winner Seattle Slew who, like Sunday Silence, had been entered in the Keeneland July sale as a yearling. But Houston, who was accepted in the select portion of the sale, had no trouble attracting a buyer. Trainer D. Wayne Lukas bid $2.9 million for the colt, making him the second highest-priced yearling sold in 1987. Sunday Silence was sold on the third day of the sale, a non-select session.

Lukas' investment began to pay dividends when he raced the horse as a two-year-old. Houston came into the Hollywood Park race off a lone victory by twelve and a half lengths in a maiden race at Belmont Park. Lukas already was touting the colt as a potential Kentucky Derby contender.

When Valenzuela pulled one of the many "no shows" that got him in trouble with owners, trainers, and racing officials, Whittingham gave Gryder a chance to ride Sunday Silence in the horse's first start against winners. Breaking from the inside post position as the 9-5 second choice in the wagering, Sunday Silence missed a beat coming out of the gate, getting away in fifth. But he quickly found his rhythm and was in contention before going a quarter-mile. He took the lead around the turn and opened up on Houston by a length and a half with a furlong to run. But Houston fought back under the veteran rider Laffit Pincay Jr. to win by a head in a very good effort by both horses.

"He was wanting to lean out on me, especially in the stretch," Gryder said of Sunday Silence. "But he was a lot better behaved than he was when I saw his first race. He ran every direction but forward that day."

Whittingham, who had won his first Kentucky Derby only two years earlier with the Nijinsky II colt Ferdinand, wanted nothing more than to capture the Run for the Roses once again. In Sunday Silence, he figured he might have the right kind of colt to take him back to Kentucky. But, as Whittingham liked to say, "You've got to climb pretty high up the tree if you want to get the ham." In other words, getting the prize was not going to be easy, and plenty of others had their eyes on it, too.

CHAPTER 5

No Easy Rival

On paper, the fifth race at Saratoga Race Course on August 19, 1988, was just another contest for two-year-old colts that had never won a race. But at this historic track in the upstate New York town of Saratoga Springs, racing journalists and fans alike watch two-year-old maiden events the way miners search for gold in a rich vein of ore. They know a precious commodity — a future racing superstar — may be close at hand.

A handsome chestnut colt named Easy Goer turned in a fourteen-karat performance in the aforementioned maiden race, drawing off down the stretch like a seasoned professional to win by two and a half lengths over a good-looking Raja Baba colt by the name of Is It True. More impressively, Easy Goer's time for the seven furlongs on a fast track, 1:22 3/5, was two and two-fifth seconds faster than another field of two-year-old maidens needed to negotiate the same distance earlier in the day.

Easy Goer's trainer, Claude R. McGaughey III, known around the racetrack as "Shug," thought his colt ran big, but the swarm of press after the race surprised him.

"All of a sudden I was surrounded by reporters wanting to talk about Easy Goer," the trainer said. "They were onto him pretty good."

It was not as if the colt's victory came as a big surprise. He was the 3-5 favorite after losing by a nose in a six-furlong maiden race earlier in the month at Belmont Park. Easy Goer was favored that day, too, at 8-5, but McGaughey later figured it took the first race for the colt "to put it all together."

Everything seemed to be coming together for McGaughey, who had been hired less than three years earlier by New York's wealthy and powerful Phipps family to be the private trainer for their high-class racing stable. When Easy Goer arrived on the scene in 1988, the native of Lexington, Kentucky, was in the midst of the best year of his professional life. He had a handful of outstanding two-year-olds, along with the crack three-year-old colt Seeking the Gold, and was nursing a four-year-old filly named Personal Ensign through a third unbeaten season. He also trained Mining, one of the top sprinters in the country, and the good older horse Personal Flag.

By the time 1988 was over, McGaughey's runners had won fifty-eight races from just 216 starts for earnings of $7,341,087. Runners trained by D. Wayne Lukas' stable had earned more than $17 million to lead North American trainers, but Lukas scattered his large public stable at tracks throughout the country and had 1,500 starters — nearly seven times the number saddled by McGaughey.

Voters who determine the sport's year-end championships, the Eclipse Awards, recognized McGaughey's accomplishments and voted him the award as outstanding trainer over Lukas. Ogden Phipps, the patriarch of the Phipps stable, was leading owner and breeder by money won in 1988. He also was voted Eclipse Awards as outstanding owner and breeder, his first since the awards were inaugurated in 1971.

It was the kind of year Phipps could only dream of when he hired McGaughey in November 1985 after suffering through several lean years. McGaughey, who attended school at the University of Mississippi before answering the call of the racetrack, got his informal education from the Hall of Fame trainer, Frank Whiteley, and his son, David. He learned his lessons well, going out on his own in 1979. A few years later he gained national attention as trainer for Loblolly Stable, whose top runner was Vanlandingham, winner of an Eclipse Award as best older horse of 1985.

The seeds for the Phipps stable were planted in 1925, when Ogden Phipps was sixteen years old. While his father, Henry Carnegie Phipps, was a polo player with little interest in racing, his mother, Gladys Mills Phipps, bought several yearlings that became the foundation for the Wheatley Stable. The stable enjoyed great success over the years, most significantly with the top-class runner Bold Ruler, Horse of the Year in 1957.

Only six years after his mother began her racing stable, young Ogden Phipps registered the black silks with cherry cap that would grace winner's circles over the next eight decades. The family stable has carried on to the next two generations, with his son, Ogden Mills "Dinny" Phipps, and several grandchildren deeply involved in the operation at the turn of the twenty-first century.

Phipps bred nearly ninety stakes winners before Easy Goer's emergence in 1988, among them Buckpasser, the Horse of the Year in 1966 who sired two other Phipps champions, the fillies Relaxing and Numbered Account.

Easy Goer was produced from one of those filly champions, Relaxing, whose third dam, Big Hurry, was acquired by Phipps in 1946 from the Idle Hour Farm of E.R. Bradley. Big Hurry was sired by Black Toney and was out of one of Thoroughbred breeding's greatest producing mares, La Troienne.

Calumet Farm's Alydar, whose losing duels to Affirmed in the 1978 Triple Crown made him a racing legend, was the sire of Easy Goer. The Phipps colt, with royalty throughout his bloodlines, was the antithesis of Sunday Silence.

The Phipps mares and foals resided at Claiborne Farm, putting Easy Goer and Sunday Silence only a few furlongs apart as they roamed the limestone-rich fields of Bourbon County in 1986 and 1987. Of course, Phipps was more than a Claiborne client. He was the adviser who is thought to have swayed the farm's trustees to turn over leadership of Claiborne to young Seth

Hancock at the expense of his older brother, Arthur.

So, while Sunday Silence went unwanted at yearling and two-year-old sales for a financially struggling
Arthur Hancock, Easy Goer was part of a well-oiled
breeding and racing machine. The son of Alydar was
welcomed with open arms at McGaughey's base early
in 1988, Payson Park, a relaxed Florida training center
west of the old-monied Palm Beach, where the Phipps
family maintains a winter home.

McGaughey first saw Easy Goer as a yearling at
Claiborne the previous June. "He was a beautiful bod-
ied horse," the trainer remembered. "He was a little
'clubby' in one foot, but they did a nice job of correct-
ing it." The club-foot condition and oversized ankles
provided a challenge to the trainer throughout Easy
Goer's racing career, but the colt also displayed enor-
mous talent that made worthwhile the extra work
required to care for him. "The ankles were a concern,"
said McGaughey, who drew upon his experience as
assistant to the Whiteleys to treat the colt.

Easy Goer shipped from Florida to Belmont Park for
the spring race meeting and stepped up his training.
"He would always do something, somewhere in his

works, that was good," McGaughey said. "It wasn't always the same thing, and it wasn't always at the same place, but he always showed you something."

After narrowly losing his first race at Belmont, Easy Goer shipped with the rest of the Phipps stable to Saratoga. He worked an easy half-mile there in :48 and then put in a five-furlong breeze in 1:00 — both on the Oklahoma training track — and McGaughey knew the colt was primed to win.

His maiden victory was Easy Goer's only Saratoga appearance. Three weeks later, during the Belmont Park fall meeting, he toyed with an allowance field, winning by five and a half lengths as a 3-5 favorite. Easy Goer's final time of 1:15 2/5 for six and a half furlongs was just two-fifths of a second off the track record. The trainer's instructions to jockey Pat Day were to "let him settle and make one run." That he did, sweeping from third to first with a breathtaking burst of speed at the top of the stretch.

By now Easy Goer was the talk of the racing world, with Turf writers, fans, and horsemen beginning to make comparisons between the big, red colt and another chestnut superstar, Secretariat, who similarly

had made a big splash during his two-year-old season in New York sixteen years earlier.

Easy Goer was the 3-10 favorite to win the grade I Cowdin Stakes at seven furlongs on October 1. He got the job done, winning by three lengths, but his performance was not nearly as brilliant as his previous race. McGaughey said his colt didn't seem to favor the dry, powdery surface that many horsemen referred to as "big sandy."

That didn't dissuade racing fans from pounding Easy Goer down to 1-10 odds in the grade I Champagne Stakes two weeks later. In that one-mile event, Easy Goer sat just off the early pace established by Is It True, then blew past that colt in the stretch, winning by four lengths and covering the distance on a fast track in 1:34 4/5.

Many viewed the Phipps colt to be as close to a cinch as can be found in racing when he was shipped to Churchill Downs for the November 5 Breeders' Cup Juvenile, a grade I event at a mile and one-sixteenth. He was bet down to 3-10, one of the heaviest favorites in the history of the championship race series.

"I went into the Breeders' Cup with a world of confidence," said McGaughey, "but nothing went right."

The 1988 Breeders' Cup was cool, dark, and damp,

with the main track rated as muddy. Easy Goer drew the number nine post position in a field of ten, which would make a short run to the first turn on a track that had a one-mile circumference. By contrast, the Champagne was a one-mile race run around one turn over the mile and a half main track at Belmont Park. Making matters worse, Easy Goer broke toward the outside in the Juvenile, bumping with Mountain Ghost and never appearing to grab hold of the slick racetrack.

Meanwhile, Is It True, a Lukas-trained colt that Easy Goer had handled easily in their previous meetings, was winging along on an uncontested lead under Laffit Pincay Jr. Easy Goer rallied from seventh position down the backstretch, swung wide at the top of the stretch, and slowly ate into Is It True's margin. But Day could not get him closer than the length and a quarter advantage Is It True maintained at the wire. It was a stunning upset, one that deflated McGaughey and the Phippses, and came just one hour after their Personal Ensign signed off on her unbeaten career with a gut-wrenching, last-second victory in the Distaff over Winning Colors and Goodbye Halo.

Despite the loss, his second in six starts, Easy Goer

easily outdistanced his contemporaries in Eclipse Award voting. Personal Ensign also was voted a championship, giving the Phipps-McGaughey team a remarkable five Eclipse Awards for the year.

McGaughey, with his long-range plans including a return to Churchill Downs on the first Saturday in May for the Kentucky Derby, decided to give Easy Goer some well-deserved time off. "His shins were starting to bug him, and the ankles were getting big," he said. "We stopped on him and fired his shins and ankles."

Easy Goer would need the rest. A new shooter out West, Sunday Silence, was just getting his career started as Easy Goer's two-year-old campaign was ending. A memorable three-year-old campaign was just around the corner.

SUNDAY SILENCE

CHAPTER 6

Rolling The Dice

T he phone started ringing at Stone Farm after Sunday Silence had wrapped up his two-year-old season in early December of 1988. Suddenly, the horse no one wanted was a hot commodity as a Kentucky Derby prospect.

One of the parties briefly interested was none other than Tom Tatham, the man who bred Sunday Silence but let him go for a paltry $17,000 as a yearling. "I made a deal to buy back into the colt, trading a number of seasons and shares to Halo for a quarter interest," said Tatham. "But we found some heat in his ankle during a veterinary inspection and the deal was off."

Other offers came in, and Arthur Hancock looked to trainer Charlie Whittingham for guidance. Goodbye Halo's outstanding season in 1988 helped reduce some of Hancock's debt, but he still had six children to feed and a big mortgage to pay.

"Charlie, I don't know what to do," Hancock said one day. "Someone's made an offer of a million dollars for my half-interest. You think I should take it?"

"I can't tell you what to do, my boy," Whittingham told him. "These are perishable commodities, like strawberries. You'll have to decide for yourself what to do."

Hancock bought some time to make his decision. A million dollars would ease his financial burden considerably, but there was no telling how good Sunday Silence might turn out to be. If only he could find out what his trainer really thought of the colt.

He made another call to Whittingham. "I'll tell you what we can do," Hancock offered. "We'll each put a quarter interest together — you and me — and split the million dollars. What do you think?"

"I'm not selling," Whittingham said, without hesitation.

Hancock got the answer he was looking for. He decided to roll the dice and retain his half-interest.

With the 1989 Kentucky Derby just over two months away, Sunday Silence debuted as a three-year-old on March 2. He went postward as a heavy favorite in a six and a half-furlong sprint at Santa Anita. The track came up sloppy that day, and Sunday Silence came up big, going wire to wire to win by four and a half lengths. With Pat Valenzuela back in the irons, Sunday Silence zipped through very fast fractions — :21 3/5 for the opening quarter-mile, :44 3/5 for the half, and 1:08 4/5 for six furlongs — en route to a final clocking of 1:15 2/5.

People were starting to take notice that Whittingham might have a colt capable of bringing him back to Churchill Downs with a Kentucky Derby prospect for the fourth time in as many years. It was a strange phenomenon for the Bald Eagle, who had just two Derby starters, Gone Fishin' in 1958 and Divine Comedy in 1960, before bringing Ferdinand to Louisville to win the roses in 1986. That Whittingham crafted his Hall of Fame credentials without being part of the three-ring circus at Churchill Downs each May spoke volumes. While other trainers were pushing two-year-olds early in their careers with the Derby as the long-term target, Whittingham took a more sensible approach, letting his horses tell him when they were ready.

If he thought he had the horse, however, Whittingham didn't shy from pointing one for the big race. In fact, as Jay Hovdey details in the biography,

Whittingham: The Story of a Thoroughbred Racing Legend (The Blood-Horse, Inc. 1993), the Bald Eagle had been just as unlucky as he had been patient when it came to the Kentucky Derby. His first champion, Porterhouse, was the future-book favorite for the 1954 Derby when he suffered bruised heels just a few weeks before the race. Three years later, a talented Whittingham-trained colt named Royal Heir was poised to join the Derby's deep talent pool that included Iron Liege, Gallant Man, Round Table, and Bold Ruler. Illness forced him off the Derby trail at the eleventh hour.

There were others. Eagle Admiral won the 1960 Fountain of Youth Stakes at Gulfstream Park for Whittingham, but injured his knee a week before the classic. In 1966, Saber Mountain was developing into a top Derby prospect when he fractured a knee finishing second in the Santa Anita Derby. A similar hand was dealt to Balzac, who in 1978 ran second to eventual Triple Crown winner Affirmed in the Santa Anita Derby and fourth to that horse in the Hollywood Derby. He came out of the latter race with a knee fracture.

Saber Mountain and Balzac both raced for California owner-breeder and oilman Howard B. Keck. Ferdinand, a chestnut-coated son of Nijinsky II bred by Keck, carried the pink and light blue silks of his wife, Elizabeth. Ferdinand was a slow developer, finishing a distant eighth in his first start, a six-furlong maiden race on September 8, 1985, at Del Mar, the seaside track north of San Diego. Whittingham brought the colt back in another maiden sprint a month later during the Oak Tree meeting at Santa Anita, and Ferdinand improved to a third-place finish. Stretched out to a mile on October 20, the colt fell just short, losing by a nose, then came back two weeks later to win impressively, moving to the lead after a half-mile and striding out to a two and a quarter-length win at a mile.

Whittingham thought enough of Ferdinand to jump him into stakes competition immediately, taking on the quick California-bred colt Snow Chief and eight other rivals in the Hollywood Futurity on December 15. Ferdinand finished a solid third behind Snow Chief while never threatening, but the Futurity was run at a mile around one turn. Whittingham believed he had a colt that would improve with age and as the race distances grew longer.

Ferdinand did not get a break during the winter,

coming back in early January to just miss as a heavy favorite in the one-mile Los Feliz Stakes, then earned his first stakes victory later that month in the mile and one-sixteenth Santa Catalina. A narrow defeat in the San Rafael Stakes kept Ferdinand on target for the Derby, but he lost some of his luster with a dull third-place finish behind Snow Chief in the one and one-eighth mile Santa Anita Derby.

Whittingham didn't seem to mind, saying the track, though officially listed as fast, was "greasy" on top and not to Ferdinand's liking. He was champing at the bit to get the colt to Kentucky.

As the Bald Eagle expected, Ferdinand flourished in the Bluegrass. Sent early to get a feel for the Churchill Downs surface, Ferdinand had two stiff workouts, giving Whittingham a world of confidence when he gave fifty-four-year-old Bill Shoemaker a leg up in the paddock. The public did not share that confidence, however, sending Ferdinand out as a 17-1 long shot for the Kentucky Derby. The speedy Snow Chief was bet down as the favorite, at odds of 2-1.

Shoemaker, riding with the verve of a man half his age, provided Whittingham and the Kecks with one of the greatest performances of his Hall of Fame career. Leaving from the inside post, Ferdinand was cut off going into the first turn and fell back to last in the sixteen-horse field. As he gained momentum and rallied around horses approaching the stretch turn, Shoemaker faced a dilemma: continue to take an overland route and lose valuable ground or dive toward the inside and hope an opening develops. In an instant, Shoemaker made his decision, making an abrupt left-hand turn just as a narrow gap miraculously opened. He scooted Ferdinand toward the hole and his colt responded with a powerful run to the wire, pulling away to win by two and a quarter lengths.

Though he never said he regretted not winning the Kentucky Derby — at least openly — Whittingham was happy to have the monkey off his back. "You tell people what business you've been in since 1934 and the first thing they ask you is, 'Did you ever win the Kentucky Derby?' " Whittingham was quoted as saying the morning after Ferdinand's victory. "When you tell them 'no,' they walk away. Now, I guess they won't. If they ask."

Whittingham enjoyed his Derby experience so much he came right back the next year with Temperate

Sil, his first Santa Anita Derby winner. But Temperate Sil got sick after shipping to Churchill Downs and never got to run. In 1988 he brought Lively One to Kentucky after the son of Halo finished second in the Santa Anita Derby. He ended up twelfth behind Winning Colors, and some people were beginning to wonder whether Whittingham had come down with a late-in-life case of "Derby fever."

Those doubts were erased in Sunday Silence's next race, the San Felipe Handicap at Santa Anita on March 19. Coming into the mile and one-sixteenth event, Sunday Silence was overshadowed by a colt named Music Merci, who had thoroughly dominated his opponents in the one-mile San Rafael Stakes, winning by nine lengths and going off as the odds-on favorite in the San Felipe.

Coming off nothing but sprint races, young horses often are overeager when they stretch out in distance for the first time. Sunday Silence was so anxious to get going when the starting gate opened that he stumbled, giving his four rivals in the race a head start. Pat Valenzuela kept a cool head, allowing the black colt to gather himself and settle into a comfortable stride. The early fractions were blazing — :22 1/5 and :45 1/5 — but by the time the field had gone a half-mile, Sunday Silence was moving along in second, four lengths behind pace-setting Yes I'm Blue. Valenzuela had Music Merci to his inside when he gunned Sunday Silence toward the lead while making his way around the final bend, and the colt quickly took command. His margin of victory was a length and three-quarters, with a fast-closing Flying Continental eating into Sunday Silence's lead in the closing yards. Chasing those fast early fractions after his awkward start may have taken a toll on Sunday Silence, who completed the distance in 1:42 3/5.

Valenzuela, who at the age of seventeen had won the Santa Anita and Hollywood derbies of 1980 with the Tartan Farm colt Codex, jumped off Sunday Silence after the San Felipe and said, "He's the best three-year-old I've ever been on."

Whittingham was more philosophical. "How good these are that he beat today we don't know," the trainer said. "Music Merci didn't run the race he ran here the other day. Right now, it looks like we'll go (to Kentucky), but you can't tell until he runs in the other

race (the Santa Anita Derby). I wouldn't say we're the favorite (for the Kentucky Derby), but we're in the top five. I've been to the Derby with worse horses."

The clear-cut Derby favorite remained Easy Goer, who had returned to the races the same week as Sunday Silence. Two days after Whittingham sent his colt out to win that March 2 allowance race, Easy Goer went postward in the seven-furlong Swale Stakes at South Florida's Gulfstream Park. The Phipps colt turned in a dazzling performance, settling far behind the early leaders and sweeping to the lead with breathtaking ease, drawing off to win by eight and three-quarter lengths.

While the paths of Sunday Silence and Easy Goer would not cross officially until the first Saturday in May at Churchill Downs, the two colts made a joint appearance on an ABC Sports telecast on April 8, when two big Kentucky Derby preps were run. It was quite a show.

Easy Goer was simply brilliant in his race, the Gotham Stakes from New York's Aqueduct racetrack. Sent off as a 1-20 favorite against four overmatched foes in a mile race around one turn, the Phipps homebred son of Alydar could not have been more impressive. Jockey Pat Day again allowed Easy Goer to settle off the lead and then asked him to run on the turn for home. Easy Goer responded with rapid acceleration, taking command at the top of the stretch and bounding away from the field to win by thirteen lengths. His final time of 1:32 2/5 was just one-fifth of a second off the world record for a mile, set in 1968 by the great champion Dr. Fager. "Incredible," said Easy Goer's trainer, Shug McGaughey.

The opposition was stronger for Sunday Silence when he went postward a short time later in the mile and one-eighth Santa Anita Derby on a sweltering Southern California day, with temperatures in the mid-nineties. The field of six included Houston, the high-priced yearling who hung a head defeat on Sunday Silence in December. Since then, the undefeated son of Seattle Slew had enhanced his reputation even further by romping to a ten and a half-length victory in the seven-furlong Bay Shore Stakes at Aqueduct in March. Fans made him the 9-10 favorite, with Sunday Silence the second choice at 2-1. Music Merci was back for a shot at redemption. Hawkster, winner of the previous year's Norfolk Stakes at Santa Anita and most recently

fourth in the Florida Derby at Gulfstream Park, added depth to the field. So did Flying Continental, who closed strongly in deep stretch against Sunday Silence in the San Felipe.

Co-owner Arthur Hancock had flown to California to see Sunday Silence run for the first time. He watched the telecast of Easy Goer's strong performance in the one-mile Gotham and asked Whittingham what he thought. "Last time I looked they ran the Kentucky Derby at a mile and a quarter," the trainer deadpanned.

It was Sunday Silence's turn to deliver his command performance. Breaking a bit awkwardly again and bumped around between horses leaving the gate, Sunday Silence quickly got into a fluid, ground-devouring stride. He sat a close third as Houston carved out fractions of :22 3/5 for the opening quarter-mile and :45 3/5 for the half, with Music Merci breathing down the leader's neck. Houston began to weaken when the field reached the far turn and Music Merci seized the advantage, the six furlongs run in a quick 1:09 3/5. But Sunday Silence and Valenzuela had him measured, going three wide around the turn and taking the lead before reaching the stretch. High above the

Santa Anita grandstand, colorful race-caller Trevor Denman declared, "I think this Derby is over."

Sunday Silence began opening up on his tired opponents when Valenzuela cracked him on the right flank with his whip. Sunday Silence reacted by scooting in toward the rail and Valenzuela shifted the stick to his left hand. He kept after the colt down the stretch as Sunday Silence pulled away to an eleven-length triumph, the largest in the fifty-two runnings of the Santa Anita Derby. His final time of 1:47 3/5 for the nine furlongs over a fast track did not threaten the track record but came within three-fifths of a second of the stakes record set by Lucky Debonair in 1965. Flying Continental closed from last to get second. Music Merci was third, with Houston a disappointing fifth.

The victory was worth $275,000 to Sunday Silence's three owners. "Now we've got enough earned to go to Kentucky," Whittingham said after the race. "I hope we'll have enough to get back."

McGaughey was invited by the ABC Sports crew at Aqueduct to watch the Santa Anita telecast with them. He was impressed by what he saw, but it wasn't just Sunday Silence's raw talent that put the thirty-eight-

year-old McGaughey on alert. The Hall of Fame train-
er calling the shots made McGaughey respect Sunday
Silence even more. "I sure wish somebody else besides
Charlie Whittingham was training that horse,"
McGaughey said.

CHAPTER 7

Silent No More

B y the time Sunday Silence and his entourage arrived in Louisville, many racing people were willing to concede the Triple Crown to his East Coast rival, Easy Goer. Las Vegas oddsmakers installed the Alydar colt the 3-5 favorite for the Derby following his eye-catching performance in the Gotham Stakes. For good measure, Shug McGaughey put one more race into his star colt before shipping to Kentucky, the April 22 Wood Memorial Stakes at Aqueduct, run at a mile and one-eighth.

Easy Goer won the race by three lengths, carrying the same 126 pounds that all starters would have to shoulder in the Derby. While his performance was not as visually impressive as it was in the Gotham, and his time, 1:50 3/5, came nowhere near the track record, Easy Goer did nothing in the Wood to discourage his ever-growing legion of supporters from proclaiming him as the sport's next super-horse.

"He came into the race an outstanding horse. He came out a budding legend," Bill Finley wrote in *The Blood-Horse* after Easy Goer's victory in the Gotham. "Easy Goer may be one of the greats," said a headline in the *Lexington Herald-Leader* newspaper that accompanied a flattering story on the Phipps' runner written by Maryjean Wall. "Is he the next Secretariat?" Turf writer Neil Milbert wrote in the *Chicago Tribune*. Easy Goer's trainer seemed to get caught up in the superlatives, proclaiming that his colt "just doesn't have a weakness."

Charlie Whittingham paid no attention to the headlines or the hype, instead concentrating on this bundle of energy and raw talent that had blossomed in less than twelve months from the equine equivalent of a juvenile delinquent into a more disciplined, yet still unpredictable, overachiever.

As he had done with Ferdinand in 1986, Whittingham sent Sunday Silence to Churchill Downs early enough to give him time to become familiar with a racing surface with a deeper, sandier composition than the ones he raced on in California. The colt had an easy five-furlong breeze at Santa Anita on April 19 — eleven days after winning the Santa Anita Derby — then was shipped to Kentucky to prepare for his show-down with Easy Goer.

Sunday Silence's first workout at Churchill Downs was a slow seven furlongs in 1:28 flat on April 24. But Pam Mabes could sense that the colt was getting stronger and stronger in his daily gallops, and Whittingham tightened the screws further with a one-mile workout on April 29, just seven days before the Derby. The track was sloppy that morning, and Sunday Silence relished the footing, going the distance under restraint in 1:39 3/5. Combined with the strong daily gallops, this work solidified the foundation of stamina that would be needed to traverse the Derby distance of a mile and one-quarter that Sunday Silence — and all the other starters — would attempt for the first time.

There is a fine line between having a horse too wound up for a big race and not quite fit enough to show his best. If anyone knew how to circle a date on a calendar and have a horse ready for a one hundred percent peak performance for that day, it was the Bald

Eagle. Three days before the Derby, Sunday Silence was like a keg of dynamite whose fuse was burning shorter and shorter. Mabes had an armful of horsepower under her that she strained to control. Sunday Silence was crying to run, and Whittingham decided to take the edge off the colt, letting him clear out his lungs the next morning, May 4, with a speedy half-mile breeze clocked in :46 3/5. The fuse was now perfectly timed for an explosion of speed and power late in the afternoon of May 6, Kentucky Derby day.

Arthur Hancock was a natural worrier, and when he saw Sunday Silence breeze so quickly on May 4, he was concerned the colt may have exerted too much energy, effectively leaving his race on the track two days early. According to Hovdey's biography of Whittingham, Hancock anxiously asked the trainer what he thought of Sunday Silence's work? "We will get the money," Whittingham told him.

A perplexed Hancock asked, "What are you saying, Charlie?"

"My boy," Whittingham responded with confidence, "we will get the money."

If Whittingham was confident on the Thursday

before the race, when entries and post positions were drawn, he was downright giddy the next day when heavy rains poured down on Louisville. The week already was miserable with damp, cold weather and hints of snow flurries, but Friday's rain put additional moisture into a racing surface that Sunday Silence already seemed to enjoy. In his only race on a wet track in California, Sunday Silence splashed his way to an easy victory over allowance competition in March.

Easy Goer, meanwhile, turned in his worst career performance the previous November on a wet and cool afternoon at Churchill Downs when he was upset by Is It True over a muddy track. His supporters had their fears of another wet track somewhat allayed on April 29 when Easy Goer scampered five furlongs through the slop in :59 flat — the fastest workout of the day at the distance. McGaughey and Whittingham were on the identical timetable, working their colts that morning and again on May 4. For his final workout two days before the race, Easy Goer also went a half-mile and was clocked in :47 flat, just two-fifths of a second slower than Sunday Silence.

While press coverage of this 115th running of the

Derby made it seem as though only two horses were in the race, the connections of thirteen other horses were willing to take a shot. First and foremost was a second runner from the Phipps' stable, this one owned by Ogden Phipps' son, Ogden Mills Phipps, known throughout the racing world as "Dinny." The colt, Awe Inspiring, was a late bloomer who had won a maiden race at two, then came on strong with a pair of victories at Hialeah Park near Miami in the Everglades Stakes in March and the Flamingo Stakes in April. Also trained by McGaughey, Awe Inspiring would run as a coupled entry in the betting with Easy Goer, though it was clear that the son's horse stood in the shadow of the chestnut-coated Easy Goer, owned by the father.

Also starting a pair of runners was trainer D. Wayne Lukas, who had sent a dozen horses postward in the Derby from 1981 to 1987 before winning the Roses for the first time with the filly Winning Colors in 1988. The best hope appeared to rest with Houston, the Seattle Slew colt so badly beaten by Sunday Silence in the Santa Anita Derby. One week before the Kentucky Derby, Houston regrouped with a five-length victory in the one-mile Derby Trial Stakes. The other Lukas entrant was Shy Tom, a son of Blushing Groom who had come to life in grass races over the winter and spring months after winning two of his first three starts on dirt in New York the previous fall.

Also in the line-up was Western Playboy, an Illinois-bred colt who had won Kentucky's two biggest Derby preps, the Jim Beam Stakes at Turfway Park in northern Kentucky and the Blue Grass Stakes at Keeneland in Lexington. The Arkansas Derby at Oaklawn Park was another big prep race, and the one-two finishers, Dansil and Clever Trevor, were sent to Churchill Downs to take on Easy Goer and Sunday Silence. Flying in from California were Flying Continental and Hawkster, both soundly thrashed by Sunday Silence in the Santa Anita Derby. Their connections believed the additional distance of the Kentucky Derby might give them a better chance in a rematch.

Easy Goer scared away most of the competition from New York, although Triple Buck, who finished third behind the Phipps' runner in the Wood Memorial, was being given another chance by his owner. From Maryland came a pair of runners, Wind Splitter and Northern Wolf, who had not been exposed

yet to top-class competition.

May 6 dawned unusually cold and damp, with temperatures in the upper thirties as some of the 122,653 fans began to arrive at Churchill Downs. While the mercury climbed to a high of fifty-one degrees, the post-time temperature of forty-three was the coldest on record for as long as such things were recorded. Steady rain dumped nine-tenths of an inch of precipitation on an already wet racetrack, making for the wettest Derby since 1967, when Proud Clarion pulled off a 30-1 upset of the great Damascus. The track condition for the 115th Derby of 1989 was listed as muddy.

Throughout the week, Whittingham fended off countless questions from reporters about Easy Goer, preferring to talk about his own colt. With the Derby now just a few hours away, Sunday Silence's trainer was asked one more time about Easy Goer by a writer from *Sports Illustrated*. "Eight million people are walking around here telling me how good Easy Goer is. Maybe they're all nuts."

Meanwhile, Easy Goer's jockey, Pat Day, was having one of the best racing afternoons of his life. Day, a

Colorado native who had become a local riding legend in his adopted home state of Kentucky, ticked off victories in five consecutive races in which he rode on the Derby program. Day could seemingly do no wrong.

The owners of fifteen horses each put up twenty-thousand dollars for the right to compete in America's most famous horse race. A sixteenth colt, Notation, was entered for the Derby but was scratched by trainer James Murphy because of the track conditions. That meant all the starters would break from the main fourteen-stall starting gate, with the exception of Northern Wolf, who was assigned post fifteen on the outside and relegated to an auxiliary gate.

The Derby starters would race for a total purse of $749,200, with the vast majority, $574,200, going to the winner. In addition, if the Derby winner went on to victory in the Preakness and Belmont Stakes for a Triple Crown sweep, his owners would be awarded a total of five million dollars as part of a sponsorship from the Chrysler automobile company. If no horse captured the Triple Crown, Chrysler would pay out a one-million-dollar bonus to the horse that had the best finishes in the three races.

When the call was made to bring the Derby horses over to the saddling paddock, groom Charles Clay grabbed Sunday Silence's lead shank and began what for many is an intense, sometimes emotional half-mile walk. Hundreds of cheering fans line the paths of the stable area that lead to the gap that opens up onto the backstretch of the racetrack. The horses then gather near the chute, where sprint races begin, and steadily leave in single file, walking near the outside rail around the clubhouse turn and toward the finish line, finally turning left into the tunnel that leads to the paddock. While many trainers and owners get caught up in the moment, gazing skyward toward the Twin Spires atop the historic grandstand or responding to the thousands of well-wishers who press up against the rail, Whittingham marched alongside Sunday Silence like a soldier. The Hall of Famer was literally hands-on, patting Sunday Silence on the left flank to calm him and keeping the green and white blanket the colt wore straight and secure.

The atmosphere in the Churchill Downs saddling area is like nothing else a young three-year-old horse will experience. The areas both inside the restricted walking ring and outside the paddock fences are jammed with people, and the air is often filled with loud whoops and hollers from the crowd. Both Sunday Silence and Easy Goer handled the challenge well, although McGaughey kept Easy Goer in his stall rather than walk him about the ring.

The order for "riders up" came, and Sunday Silence stood stoically, his ears straight up and his eyes wandering as if attempting to soak in all the atmosphere before going on to his day's work. Whittingham lifted twenty-six-year-old Patrick Valenzuela into the saddle and gave his Derby colt one last slap on the rump. Sunday Silence pranced around the walking ring one last time before disappearing into the tunnel as a band struck up the traditional Derby song, "My Old Kentucky Home."

The walk from the paddock up to the clubhouse's third-floor box seats, where most owners and trainers watch the races, takes just a minute or two on a typical racing day at Churchill Downs. But on Derby day, with every nook and cranny bursting with humanity, people with horses racing in the Derby sometimes worry that they won't get back to their vantage point before the big race begins.

That wasn't a problem for owners and trainers of starters in the 1989 Derby. Shortly after the post parade began, Triple Buck somehow loosened one of his horseshoes, and he was hustled back to the paddock where a farrier quickly pounded it back into place. The riders of the other Derby starters were given permission to dismount, temporarily taking the weight off the backs of the horses, which were then led around by outriders. The sight of fifteen jockeys standing on the racetrack on the stretch turn of any race was an unusual one, but especially so before the biggest race of the year. The last-minute repairs to Triple Buck delayed the start by nine minutes, leaving some of the horses, including Easy Goer, slightly agitated by the time the jockeys were told to remount.

Once Triple Buck rejoined his rivals on the racetrack, the field quickly loaded into the gate, situated at the top of the long Churchill Downs stretch. Easy Goer and stablemate Awe Inspiring, the heavy favorites at odds of 4-5, broke from the thirteen and twelve posts, respectively. Sunday Silence, second choice at 3-1, was in the number ten post. Houston, coupled with Shy Tom, was third in the betting at 5-1 and started from the sixth post. Western Playboy was next in the wagering at 9-1, and none of the others were lower than 27-1 odds.

When the gates opened to the roar of the crowd, Sunday Silence ducked to his immediate left, sandwiching Triple Buck in the next stall and bumping solidly into another rival, Faultless Ensign, who was two stalls over. Valenzuela quickly straightened Sunday Silence out and claimed a forward position behind the speedy Houston, who left the gate smoothly, and two other opponents. Easy Goer left in good order but soon encountered trouble caused by Northern Wolf, who was to his outside.

Ridden by Jo Jo Ladner, Northern Wolf was a front-running colt who was expected to be among the horses competing for the early lead. Ladner, who was blind in one eye and riding in his first Derby, quickly hustled the Maryland-bred out of the gate and steered him toward the inside in the opening furlong. Ladner didn't realize that his mount had not gained a clear advantage over Easy Goer, however, and as he came inward, Day had to put the brakes on Easy Goer, just before passing the finish line the first time. Northern Wolf then leaned into Dansil, who, in turn, bumped Sunday

Silence. ABC Sports commentator Jim McKay later compared the early portion of the race to a rodeo ride.

Sunday Silence and Easy Goer recovered quickly, and both were in good position as the field rounded the clubhouse turn. Houston led the way, with an opening quarter-mile in :23 flat, and he was followed by Oklahoma-bred long shot Clever Trevor and Northern Wolf. Sunday Silence was in fourth along the inside, with Easy Goer just a half-length back and to his outside.

It was right where Day wanted Easy Goer to be. "Sunday Silence was the horse to beat," Day said later, "and I wanted to stay in contact with him."

The positions were largely unchanged as the field made its way around the turn and down the backstretch. Houston continued to click off the fractions, going a half-mile in :46 3/5 and six furlongs in 1:11 2/5. Valenzuela bided his time as Sunday Silence galloped smoothly along, racing five or six lengths behind Houston and one to two lengths ahead of Easy Goer.

Then, with less than a half-mile to run, Valenzuela asked Sunday Silence to make his move. He shifted to the outside and took aim on the leaders. Day could sense that his colt was not moving nearly as easily as Sunday

Silence, who was gliding toward the front with little effort. Day began scrubbing on Easy Goer's neck and applied a steady left-handed whip around the final turn. Valenzuela had barely moved his hands on Sunday Silence. "My horse just wasn't there," Day said.

Rounding into the stretch, with just a quarter-mile to the wire, Sunday Silence swung to the outside. Clever Trevor had already retreated toward the back of the pack, and Houston predictably was beginning to shorten strides. Northern Wolf was the only horse Sunday Silence had to overtake.

After Valenzuela straightened his mount at the top of the stretch, he cracked the black colt on the right flank with his whip, and Sunday Silence veered left, just as he had done when leaving the starting gate, and now was shoulder to shoulder with Northern Wolf. "He shied from the noise of the crowd," his rider said.

Valenzuela shifted the stick to his left hand and applied it several times. Sunday Silence responded by careening in the opposite direction. But now he was clear of Northern Wolf, a length and one-half in front with only a furlong to run. No one appeared to be closing in on the new leader. Day shifted to right-handed

strokes of the whip on Easy Goer, but he seemed to be spinning his wheels, barely able to outrun stablemate Awe Inspiring.

Sunday Silence continued his zigzag route to the wire, moving left when struck with a right-handed whip and ducking right when hit on the left side. Valenzuela wrapped Sunday Silence up in the final sixteenth of a mile and waved the stick triumphantly at the wire. He was clear by two and one-half lengths. Easy Goer finished a head in front of Awe Inspiring, with Dansil three-quarters of a length back in fourth. Hawkster finished fifth, followed by Northern Wolf, Irish Actor, Houston, Triple Buck, Shy Tom, Wind Splitter, Flying Continental, Clever Trevor, Faultless Ensign, and Western Playboy.

Up in the clubhouse boxes, Whittingham's wife, Peggy, was jumping up and down with joy while her husband snapped the fingers of his right hand, impatiently waiting for his horse to reach the finish. A broad smile broke out on Arthur Hancock's face as he slapped his trainer on the back in congratulations. Whittingham merely tugged on the narrow brim of the pork-pie hat pulled down low on his shiny head, as if to say, "It was nothing."

To the naked eye, the stretch run played out in an almost slow-motion sequence. A look at the clock on the tote board showed why. The final time of 2:05 was the slowest since 1958, when Tim Tam won the Derby in the same time, also on a muddy track. With a mile clocking of 1:37 4/5, Sunday Silence ran his final quarter-mile in a very tedious twenty-seven seconds. His supporters were rewarded with an $8.20 win mutuel on a two-dollar bet.

Neither the time of the race nor the fashion of Sunday Silence's triumphant stretch run could tarnish the victory in the eyes of the colt's owners. "It's one of the greatest days of my life," Hancock said on the victory stand in the track's infield.

Valenzuela dedicated the win to Joe Manzi, a California trainer who had supported him through good times and bad during his checkered career. Manzi had died suddenly of a heart attack shortly before the Derby. The rider also urged the youth of America to "say no to drugs," something that Valenzuela, unfortunately, had a difficult time doing.

Whittingham made a bold prediction when asked on national television if Sunday Silence would go on to

the Preakness. "If ever a horse can go all the way, this one can," Whittingham said. "We'll be another Triple Crown winner."

SUNDAY SILENCE

CHAPTER 8

R-E-S-P-E-C-T

O n Derby night, when Charlie and Peggy Whittingham led an entourage into the restaurant at their Louisville hotel, the Executive West, diners gave them a standing ovation. Whittingham was a beloved figure in racing who many people felt was getting his just deserts — two Derby triumphs in four years — after a lifetime of achievement and dedication to the sport.

He was more than a fine horseman, however. Despite a sometimes rough exterior and a rambunctious reputation, Whittingham was a class act. The next morning, he paid a visit to Shug McGaughey to offer his condolences for Easy Goer's defeat.

The gesture was similar to the one Whittingham would make five years later, when his charge, Strodes Creek, finished second in the 120th Kentucky Derby behind Go for Gin. The morning after the defeat,

Whittingham paid his respects to winning trainer Nick Zito, stopping by his barn for a private chat. "Now you know, this is an honor," Zito said of the visit. "When the king walks toward the prince, this is an honor."

McGaughey, a Kentucky native who called the Derby "the ultimate dream," was disappointed in the loss but not devastated. Coming off a year when horses he trained won fifteen grade I races, McGaughey could have been forgiven for thinking this was an easy game and that he'd have a steady stream of horses that would contend for the roses. "I thought we'd do this every year," he thought at the time.

But nothing in racing is predictable, or easy. The Sunday Silence camp would be reminded of that just one week after the Kentucky Derby as their colt trained for the Triple Crown's second leg, the Preakness Stakes.

Sunday Silence was shipped to Pimlico racecourse in Baltimore, without incident and took up residence in stall forty in the stakes barn, the one traditionally reserved for the Kentucky Derby winner. Everything was going smoothly until the afternoon of May 13 when Sunday Silence started favoring his right front foot after a routine gallop under exercise rider Pam

Mabes earlier in the day. Whittingham surmised the colt must have stepped on something on the racetrack that bruised his foot.

At five o'clock the next morning, after Sunday Silence's condition failed to improve, Whittingham called Dr. Alex Harthill, whose veterinary office was across the street from Churchill Downs in Louisville. Harthill, whose expertise with good horses had earned him the nickname "Derby Doctor," caught the next flight to Baltimore and was at Pimlico by nine o'clock the same morning to examine the Derby winner.

Harthill's conclusion? The Derby winner was lame, due to a bruised foot or hematoma. The technical term was a subsolar abscess. The good news was that the injured area had not become infected or formed a pus pocket, which would have complicated the situation and made it virtually impossible for any horse to race within a week.

Harthill prescribed what he called "conventional treatment," soaking the foot in Epsom salts in an effort to increase the blood circulation in the affected area. He then painted the injured foot with a mixture of turpentine and iodine to seal it. A poultice consisting of more

turpentine, iodine, and an anti-inflammatory agent known as antiphlogistine was wrapped around the area.

"The key is to keep the circulation going. That's the key to almost anything in medicine," Harthill told *The Blood-Horse*. "You've got to get the diseased blood away, and the only way you can do that is with a dilution process — bringing in fresh oxygenated blood.

"The Epsom salts keeps the hoof wall from becoming waterlogged. The turpentine drives the quick back, drives the sensitive area back."

Sunday Silence was not able to go to the racetrack on the Sunday or Monday before Saturday's Preakness. Whittingham had the colt walked around the shed row each morning and afternoon so that he was not completely void of exercise.

Harthill also concluded that Sunday Silence would need new horseshoes on both front feet. He outlined a pattern of the feet on a sheet of paper and faxed it to Dr. Ric Redden, an equine foot specialist based outside of Lexington. Redden and an associate, farrier Joe Carroll, prepared several sets of aluminum bar shoes and took them, along with a portable X-ray machine, with them on a private jet to Baltimore.

There are different kinds of bar shoes used to protect sensitive or injured feet. In the case of Sunday Silence, Carroll and Redden used an "egg" bar shoe, which is a conventional racing plate with a straight bar connecting the two heels of the shoe. The purpose of the shoe is to protect the injured part of a horse's foot from the concussion caused when the foot hits the ground. While Sunday Silence's left foot was not injured, an identical shoe was put on that foot so there would be no imbalance. In addition to the bar shoes, Carroll and Redden applied pads between the shoe and foot to further absorb the concussion.

"The shoe picks up frog pressure," Carroll told *The Blood-Horse*. "The frog is a supportive structure of the foot. When a horse gets sore in the walls, you must pick up weight somewhere else to redistribute the weight."

Whittingham called Arthur Hancock at Stone Farm to alert him to the problem that potentially could prevent Sunday Silence from running in the Preakness. "I could tell by the tone of Charlie's voice it might be pretty rough," Hancock told *The Blood-Horse* at the time. "He thought maybe he might have a wing frac-

ture. I tell you, it was 'Sunday silence' that day. It was pretty gloomy for a while."

Fortunately, X-rays proved fears of any fracture to be unfounded.

Groom Charles Clay spent several nights in Sunday Silence's stall, soaking the injured foot and then ensuring that the poultice stayed on the injured area. He caught a few winks whenever possible.

Clay, fifty-one, had worked in the Whittingham barn for a number of years, handling such top horses as champion grass mare Estrapade, among others. A native of Washington, D.C., Clay left home at the age of fourteen to work on the backstretch of racetracks in the Mid-Atlantic region, his first job coming at Charles Town in West Virginia. He took a cross-country train some years later, and California became his home. "I saw the weather and the beautiful women and said there's no going back," he told Louisville's *Courier-Journal* newspaper.

The treatment worked, but time was running short. Whittingham knew he had to get Sunday Silence back onto the racetrack, and on Tuesday, four days before the May 20 Preakness, he gave Mabes a leg up and then held his breath while she took him through his paces.

Mabes was just as worried as Whittingham, but her concern quickly turned to delight. "After walking for two days under tack, he was the strongest and most joyful I'd ever felt him before," she said. "There wasn't a hint of anything wrong with his feet. He was just leaping for joy. The track was soft and damp, and he was just ecstatic. It sent chills up and down my spine. I knew this horse was just fine."

Sunday Silence was feeling so good, in fact, that he reverted to some of the bad habits he had displayed during his training hours as a two-year-old. One of those bad habits was a propensity to act studdish and mount the ponies that would accompany him to and from the racetrack. "We solved that problem eventually," Mabes said. "He loved peppermints, and whoever was on the pony would rattle the peppermint wrappers to get his attention. He'd hear the sound of the paper, take the peppermint from the pony rider, and as he ate the mint, the pony rider would snap a chain over him."

At Pimlico, an unsuspecting pony rider went to get Sunday Silence and bring him back to the barn after his gallop. "It was awful," Mabes said. "He jumped in the air and mounted the pony in broad daylight, with all the cameras on him. He had both of his legs wrapped around the pony girl. I had to jog Sunday Silence back to the barn by myself."

Sunday Silence worked a half-mile in :47 1/5 on Thursday morning and on Friday, the morning before the Preakness, the bars were filed off Sunday Silence's customized shoes. All systems were "go."

McGaughey sent Easy Goer back to New York and the peace and quiet of his barn at Belmont Park, where he trained for the Preakness. Sunday Silence was in one of racing's most notorious goldfish bowls, the stakes barn of Pimlico, where hundreds of writers, television camera crews, and tourists gather each morning of Preakness week. A growing number of those writers and camera crews loitered directly in front of Sunday Silence's stall, and his groom's patience was wearing thin. Clay felt the colt was getting agitated from all the attention. "I can't keep you people from hanging around," he muttered, according to Jay Hovdey in his biography of Whittingham. "But I sure as hell can remove the view." Clay then closed the doors on Sunday Silence's stall to give the colt some privacy.

The press reacted with skepticism, largely because many of them were suspicious of Harthill, a vet whose magic touch with horses was thought by some to be just a little too magical. The closed doors, some of them suspected, meant something illegal could be going on inside, especially when Harthill was in the stall.

Pete Axthelm, a well-known writer and broadcaster who was chief among the cynics in the press the week of the Preakness, conducted an interview with Harthill the day of the race, saying there was "a lot of mystery behind Sunday Silence."

When Harthill explained Sunday Silence's injury to Axthelm and said it was treated "conventionally," Axthelm laughed. A clearly agitated Harthill told Axthelm the colt's stall doors were closed because "we were trying to protect him from you guys."

In fact, Sunday Silence was the only Kentucky Derby starter who wasn't treated with Lasix or Butazolidin, the two permitted medications that are reported to the public by way of the track programs. Lasix is used to treat a common affliction in horses known as exercised-induced pulmonary hemorrhage. Butazolidin, or Bute, is an anti-inflammatory. Easy

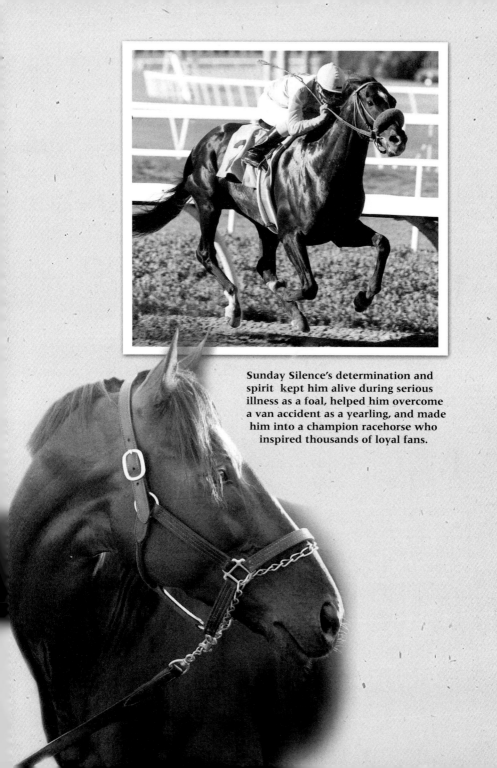

Sunday Silence's determination and spirit kept him alive during serious illness as a foal, helped him overcome a van accident as a yearling, and made him into a champion racehorse who inspired thousands of loyal fans.

Sunday Silence received his tempestuous nature from his sire, Halo (top), and his speed from his grandsire, champion Hail to Reason (above). Undistinguished as a racehorse and as a stallion, Understanding (right) did make one important mark — as the sire of Wishing Well, dam of Sunday Silence (below with her famous offspring).

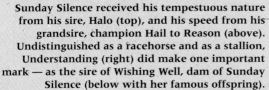

Arthur Hancock III grew up in the shadow of his grandfather, A.B. Hancock Sr., and father, Bull Hancock (left, Hancock as a boy, with his father, standing, and grandfather), and expected to follow them in running his family's storied Claiborne Farm. When that didn't happen, Hancock went out on his own and established Stone Farm. Hancock and his wife, Staci (below), have since enjoyed many successes, with Sunday Silence foremost among them.

Breeder Tom Tatham (below right) let Sunday Silence go to Arthur Hancock for $17,000. Later Hancock found a less-than-silent partner in trainer Charlie Whittingham (left, telling Sunday Silence to be quiet), who brought in his friend, Dr. Ernest Gaillard (below left), as another partner.

Patrick Valenzuela (below), a talented jockey plagued by substance abuse problems, rode Sunday Silence in all but two of the colt's fourteen races. Chris McCarron (above with Whittingham) was aboard for Sunday Silence's Breeders' Cup Classic win.

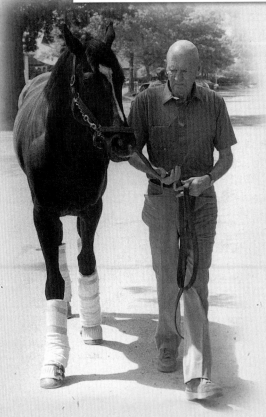

A gangly and spirited youth, Sunday Silence challenged his trainer during his early lessons on the racetrack. His talent was evident in a ten-length maiden victory, but his inexperience cost him a close battle with Houston in their final start as two-year-olds.

Sunday Silence proved he could handle two turns in winning the San Felipe Stakes (above), then turned in a powerhouse performance to win the Santa Anita Derby by eleven lengths (top left). After the race, Valenzuela celebrated aboard his Kentucky Derby-bound colt.

Whittingham sent Sunday Silence to Churchill Downs early to familiarize the colt with the track (top). Although second choice to East Coast star Easy Goer, Sunday Silence was all alone at the finish of the Kentucky Derby (above). In the winner's circle, Staci Hancock and Peggy Whittingham (right) showed off their new Derby accessory — a blanket of roses.

Sunday Silence and Easy Goer were back for Round 2 in the Preakness. The two battled neck and neck down the stretch, their strides perfectly matched, in one of racing's most thrilling finishes. At the wire, Sunday Silence edged his chestnut rival by a nose.

In the paddock before the Belmont Stakes, Sunday Silence (right with groom Charles Clay) appeared ready for his chance at Triple Crown glory. But Belmont Park belonged to Easy Goer and so did the race. Easy Goer (below, heading into the stretch) won easily by eight lengths, with Sunday Silence holding for second.

Returned to California, Sunday Silence came up short to Prized in the Swaps Stakes (below), but returned to form to win the Super Derby (right) by six lengths. Sunday Silence met old rival Easy Goer for one final bout in the Breeders' Cup Classic. The black colt got the win and Horse of the Year honors.

Sunday Silence, with regular exercise rider Pam Mabes aboard, began preparing for his four-year-old season after undergoing arthroscopic knee surgery in November. He also returned with a new co-owner — Zenya Yoshida of Shadai Farm (below, right), shown with son Teruya (left) and Arthur Hancock.

Sunday Silence made his four-year-old debut in the Californian Stakes at Hollywood Park in June of 1990 and won wire to wire (above). Three weeks later, though, he fell just short to eventual Horse of the Year Criminal Type in the Hollywood Gold Cup (below). It was Sunday Silence's last race. He was retired shortly after, when a torn ligament in his left front ankle was discovered.

Upon his retirement, Sunday Silence was sent to Hancock's Stone Farm (above), where he posed for a conformation shot. He was to enter stud there, but little interest from American breeders and a generous offer from abroad soon had Sunday Silence on his way to Japan.

In the fall of 1990, Zenya Yoshida purchased Sunday Silence from Arthur Hancock and partners. The champion colt entered stud at Yoshida's Shadai Farm on the island of Hokkaido, Japan, in early spring of 1991 (above and below).

Sunday Silence finally got some respect when he was inducted into the Racing Hall of Fame in 1996.

Sunday Silence has dominated the stallion ranks in Japan. His offspring have won most of the country's major races. His top performers include, top to bottom, 2000 Japan Derby winner Agnes Flight (on left), 1995 Japan Derby winner Tayasu Tsuyoshi, and 1995 Japan Oaks winner Dance Partner.

Goer, whose owner, Ogden Phipps, was a longtime opponent of race-day medication in horses, was treated with Bute on the morning of the Derby.

McGaughey speculated the Bute might have dulled Easy Goer in the Derby and decided not to give it to the horse in Baltimore. He also thought the track condition at Churchill Downs led to Easy Goer's uncharacteristically poor performance. In fact, McGaughey said he would not run Easy Goer in the Preakness if the track came up sloppy or muddy. But after thirteen consecutive days of rain, Preakness morning dawned warm and bright. By post time it was a breezy eighty-eight degrees and the track was lightning fast.

A Pimlico record crowd of 90,145 turned out for the May 20 rematch between Sunday Silence and Easy Goer. Perhaps swayed by the preponderance of support for Easy Goer among racing writers who continued to think the son of Alydar was the better horse, the fans made Easy Goer the 3-5 favorite. Sunday Silence was the second betting choice at 2-1.

In a poll of racing writers published in the *Baltimore Sun* newspaper, Easy Goer was picked to win by forty-five writers. Only twelve of those asked picked Sunday

Silence. Arthur Hancock couldn't figure out why his horse was being slighted. The black sheep of the Hancock family seemed to be passing on his reputation to the Kentucky Derby winner.

The six other horses who entered this 114th running of the Preakness seemed like bit players. Houston was back for another try, trainer D. Wayne Lukas thinking the colt might find the racing surface at Pimlico more conducive to his front-running style. Other Derby starters in the Preakness line-up included Dansil, Northern Wolf, and Hawkster, the latter of whom also missed some training because of a foot injury. Two new-comers joined the fray, Rock Point from New York and Pulverizing from Maryland, but neither was given much of a chance at stealing the stage from Sunday Silence and Easy Goer. In fact, Houston, at odds of 5-1, was the only other horse sent away at odds under 20-1.

Sunday Silence broke from the number seven post position and was bumped coming out of the gate by Northern Wolf, who started from the outside gate. Easy Goer left the gate a step slowly from the number two post and settled in along the rail as the field made its way down the Pimlico stretch for the first time.

As expected, Northern Wolf and Houston battled for the early advantage, with Angel Cordero Jr. and Houston eventually seizing command. After an opening quarter-mile in :23 2/5, Houston put daylight between himself and the others, leading by two and a half lengths through a :46 2/5 half-mile. But the real race was taking place behind him.

Patrick Valenzuela put Sunday Silence into third position as the field rounded the turn, behind Houston and Northern Wolf and just outside of Pulverizing. Easy Goer was several lengths behind in fifth position. As the horses traveled down the backstretch, however, Day revved up the big red engine beneath him and sent Easy Goer toward the lead. Valenzuela took a peek over his right shoulder and saw the black and cherry colors of the Phipps stable fast approaching. But Day had gotten the jump on him and had Valenzuela in a trap, just behind a tiring Houston and directly to Easy Goer's inside.

With a half-mile to run, Easy Goer zoomed past Houston and Sunday Silence. Valenzuela momentarily checked his mount, losing valuable momentum.

A tremendous cheer went up from the crowd as Easy

Goer opened up a clear advantage on Sunday Silence after six furlongs had been run in a blazing 1:09 3/5.

But Sunday Silence was far from finished. Valenzuela put him back into high gear and he quickly made up the lost ground around the turn. When the two colts hit the top of the stretch, with Easy Goer on the rail and Sunday Silence just to his outside, the Derby winner had regained a narrow advantage. Trevor Denman, the California race commentator who had been brought in to call the Preakness, shouted, "Here's the race we've been waiting for!"

Easy Goer was braced for the challenge. After moving so suddenly to the lead, Day eased up on Easy Goer, wanting to save something for a stretch battle. The two jockeys went to work, Day whipping Easy Goer with his left hand and Valenzuela working Sunday Silence over with his right. They covered the opening mile in 1:34 1/5.

Stride for stride they went, almost in unison, neither willing to give an inch. Valenzuela pinned Day and Easy Goer in tight quarters along the rail. Day felt the pressure and tugged on the right reins, jerking Easy Goer's head to the right, wanting him to look his opponent in the eye and fight him off.

In the final seventy yards, Valenzuela put away his whip and nudged Sunday Silence with an aggressive hand ride. Day did the same. Both horses strained for the wire, their strides perfectly matched. But Sunday Silence got the nod, edging away in the final yards to win by a few inches.

Valenzuela waved his whip in celebration, but even those at the finish line had trouble separating the two colts. Mabes and Harthill watched the race together on the porch in front of the jockeys' room, right at the wire. Neither could tell who had won. As Whittingham made his way past them on the way to the track, Mabes said, "Charlie, I don't know..." "Shut up, girl," he told her. "We got it."

"I grabbed (Charles) Clay's hand, and he and I went hand and hand into the winner's circle," Mabes said.

On ABC's broadcast of the race, Jim McKay conducted a brief interview with Valenzuela, who was still on horseback. The outrider who picked up Sunday Silence after the race was carrying a microphone. "What do you think, Pat? Did you win?" he asked him. "I think so," Valenzuela said. "Pat tried to screw me the whole way around, but he couldn't do it."

Valenzuela was referring to Day's tactics that put
Sunday Silence in a box approaching the far turn and
the way he pulled Easy Goer off the rail in deep stretch.
But Day filed an objection with the stewards, claiming
Sunday Silence interfered with him down the stretch.

The three track stewards reviewed the videotapes of
the race, including a head-on shot of the stretch run,
and disallowed the claim. Steward John Heisler told
the *Baltimore Sun*. "There's no way I could take that
horse down. The way Valenzuela rode Sunday Silence
is the name of the game. For that kind of money at
stake, you'd better be riding your butt off."

The official margin was a nose. It was another five
lengths back to the third-place finisher, Rock Point.
After completing the slowest Derby in thirty years,
Sunday Silence had run the third-fastest Preakness,
covering a mile and three-sixteenths in 1:53 4/5.

"Easy Goer is a great horse, and it's a shame someone had to lose," Hancock said in winner's circle ceremonies. Then, baring some of the sting he had felt from
the lack of respect shown his horse, Hancock quoted
from William Cullen Bryant's poem, *The Battle-Field*.

"Truth crushed to Earth shall rise again,

The eternal years of God are hers;

But Error, wounded, writhes with pain,

And dies among his worshipers."

A few minutes later, Hancock was quoting a different verse. Arriving in the press box for post-race interviews, he began with a few bars from the hit song of Aretha Franklin: "R-E-S-P-E-C-T, find out what it means to me."

He wasn't done, challenging the press further about Easy Goer. "I'd like to ask you a question," he said. "Was it a little too dry today? Too moist? Too hot? Too windy? I'm not resentful, but I'm proud of our horse and I want him to have the respect he deserves."

Sunday Silence was now just one race away from becoming racing's twelfth Triple Crown winner. But the Belmont Stakes, at a mile and one-half, was not just the longest and most demanding of the three races. It would take place in Easy Goer's backyard, Belmont Park, where the Phipps family and McGaughey had enjoyed their greatest success.

SUNDAY SILENCE

CHAPTER 9

Easy Does It

S unday Silence and Easy Goer had barely crossed the finish line in the Preakness before comparisons were being made with Affirmed and Alydar, the two great rivals of the 1978 Triple Crown.

Unlike Sunday Silence, Affirmed was a seasoned campaigner as a juvenile, winning seven of nine starts and being awarded an Eclipse Award as top two-year-old colt or gelding. His rivalry with Alydar began during the summer of his two-year-old year, but at season's end Affirmed shipped to the West Coast stable of trainer Lazaro Barrera while Alydar was sent to Florida with other Calumet Farm runners trained by John Veitch.

Both horses arrived at Churchill Downs unbeaten for the year and coming off impressive victories, Affirmed in the Hollywood Derby at Hollywood Park and Alydar in Keeneland's Blue Grass Stakes. Fans made Alydar the 6-5 Kentucky Derby favorite, apparently thinking the son of Raise a Native's late-running style was better suited to the classic American distance of ten furlongs. Affirmed, a Florida-bred product of Louis and Patrice Wolfson's Harbor View Farm, was a precocious colt, full of early speed. Skeptics thought the colt by Raise a Native's son, Exclusive Native, would not have the stamina required to win. Affirmed was the 9-5 second choice.

But Affirmed prevailed in the Kentucky Derby, holding off a late charge by Alydar to win by a length and a half. He similarly captured the Preakness, winning by a neck. When the two colts arrived at Belmont Park for the Triple Crown's final leg, Veitch decided to remove the blinkers that Alydar had worn since August of his two-year-old season, reasoning that he might fight harder if he could look his opponent in the eye.

In the Belmont Affirmed and Alydar put on one of the great performances of all time, hooking up midway down the backstretch and dueling from there to the wire. Alydar, with veteran jockey Jorge Velasquez, raced just to the outside of Affirmed, who was ridden by the young apprentice Steve Cauthen. In the final furlong of this mile and a half classic, Alydar appeared to have all the momentum, taking the lead from Affirmed momentarily. But Cauthen switched his stick to the left hand and urged his mount on like he'd never done before. Affirmed dug in relentlessly, stretching his chestnut neck out and straining for the finish. He got there a head in front of Alydar, becoming only the eleventh Triple Crown winner in history and the third in six years, following Secretariat in 1973 and Seattle Slew in 1977.

Alydar became a footnote in history as the horse that came closest to winning the Triple Crown without capturing any one of the three races. It seemed fitting to some that Easy Goer's sire was Alydar.

In the ten years since Affirmed, three horses had come to the Belmont with a chance at Triple Crown glory.

In 1979 the brash trainer Buddy Delp won the Kentucky Derby and Preakness with Spectacular Bid. He was "the best horse to ever look through a bridle," his trainer claimed. But a poor ride by inexperienced Ronnie Franklin and a safety pin reportedly stuck by accident in the colt's foot that morning cost Spectacular Bid the Belmont.

In 1981 Pleasant Colony ground out victories in the Derby and Preakness for New York-based trainer John Campo before coming up short in the Belmont. He finished third behind Summing and Highland Blade.

Alysheba captured the Derby and Preakness in 1987 and was the first horse to have a chance at winning $5 million with a Triple Crown sweep. But the Jack Van Berg-trained runner, like Easy Goer a son of Alydar, finished fourth in the Belmont, also blowing the million-dollar bonus that went to the horse with the most points earned for top three finishes in the three races. The bonus went to Kentucky Derby and Preakness runner-up Bet Twice, who drew off by fourteen and one-quarter lengths to win the Belmont.

None of the Triple Crown attempts since 1978 captured the imagination of the racing public the way the Sunday Silence-Easy Goer rivalry did. Fueled by strong differences of opinion between racing writers from the East and West coasts, public debate always seemed to favor Easy Goer. Perhaps it was because the Triple Crown races all took place east of the Mississippi River or the simple fact that more East Coast newspapers covered horse racing. Sunday Silence never seemed to get his due.

Arthur Hancock's rendition of "Respect" did not go down well among those in Easy Goer's corner. Neither did Charlie Whittingham's confidence in Sunday Silence, which some interpreted as arrogance. Questions persisted about veterinarian Alex Harthill and the treatment he prescribed for Sunday Silence in Baltimore. Pete Axthelm, who laughed at Harthill's comment about "conventional" treatment while interviewing him on ESPN, pressed Whittingham during a televised interview before the Belmont. When New Yorker Axthelm asked Whittingham about the closed stall doors at Pimlico, Whittingham shook with anger. "The real story is you people out East can't stand the fact the other horse is getting beat," he snapped, "so you've got to have an excuse."

Adding fuel to the fire was the ban by New York racing authorities on Harthill, who was not allowed on the backstretch at Belmont Park. "That's an insult to him and an insult to me," said Whittingham, who threatened to skip Saratoga's Travers Stakes later that year because of the ban on Harthill. "That horse has probably run on less medication than any horse here," he said of Sunday Silence.

Sunday Silence exited the Preakness without any signs of lameness in the foot that gave his connections such a scare. Whittingham, who had won more races requiring a horse's stamina than any other trainer in the history of the sport, continued to put Sunday Silence through a program of two- to three-mile daily gallops. Sunday Silence had a one-mile breeze ten days before the Belmont and a three-furlong blowout on the Tuesday of Belmont week. While he had set records winning races like the mile and three-quarters San Juan Capistrano fourteen times, Whittingham had never brought a horse to the mile and a half Belmont after victories in the Kentucky Derby and Preakness.

Charles Clay, Sunday Silence's groom, confided to those around him that he was concerned the gallops were wearing on the colt rather than building his stamina. New York's weather was unseasonably hot and steamy, and tensions around Sunday Silence were rising with the temperatures.

Arthur Hancock, meanwhile, was basking in the spotlight Sunday Silence brought him. Back at Stone Farm, film crews from ABC, ESPN, and CBS arrived to help tell the story of Hancock and the horse nobody wanted. Hancock, whose flirtation with Bluegrass music included a 1981 album called *Horse of a Different Color*, made a television appearance on the popular country music show *Nashville Now* on the Monday of Belmont week. He lugged his guitar to New York to perform on *Late Night With David Letterman*. Hancock even wrote a song, "Sunday Silence," in honor of his star colt.

When all the dreams I dream do not come true
And the friends I have turn out to be so few
When it seems the world is closing in on me
Sunday Silence soothes my soul and sets me free

Every time things seem to turn out
Something else comes up to put me down
And while I do the best I can do
Sunday Silence gives me strength to make it through

Here comes Sunday Silence again
On the track of life sometimes you lose, sometimes you win
We all need a guiding hand to help us now and then
Here comes Sunday Silence again

Every now and then it's hard to face
There is no easy goin' in life's race
And when I'm feeling down and in defeat
The sound of Sunday Silence sure is sweet

Here comes Sunday Silence again
On the track of life sometimes you lose, sometimes you win
We all need a guiding hand to help us now and then
Here comes Sunday Silence again

How my race will end Lord only knows
But when Sunday's here it's time to smell the rose
And stop and count the blessings that abound
In a place where Sunday Silence can be found

Here comes Sunday Silence again
On the track of life sometimes you lose, sometimes you win
We all need a guiding hand to help us now and then
Here comes Sunday Silence
It's time for Sunday Silence
Here comes Sunday Silence again

"Stormy Weather" might have been a more appropriate song during the days immediately preceding the Belmont. Thunderstorms punctuated the region throughout the week, followed by a long, steady downpour that dumped three inches of rain on Belmont Park the day before the race. While the seeming assurance of a wet track boosted Whittingham's confidence even further, Easy Goer's trainer, Shug McGaughey, vowed to run his colt in the Belmont rain or shine.

Sunday Silence gave photographers a spectacular photo opportunity on the morning before the race on his way to what was to be a routine gallop. As Whittingham led the colt from the paddock into the tunnel under the grandstand and out onto the racetrack, Sunday Silence reared high into the air. On his way up, his left foot grazed Whittingham's skull. Whittingham was dazed, while a shocked exercise rider, Pam Mabes, did her best to hang on as Sunday Silence pawed toward the sky.

In his biography of Whittingham, Jay Hovdey wrote that Mabes cried out, "Oh my God, Charlie, are you okay?" Whittingham, who clung to the lead shank until Sunday Silence settled back on the ground, final-

ly let him go. "Go on with him, go dammit. Go on!"

The blow left only a superficial cut and bruise near Whittingham's right temple. His wife, Peggy, managed to laugh the incident off, referring to her husband's penchant for butting heads with people in his younger days. "After all his years of head-butting, he's got so much scar tissue up there you can't hurt him," she said. For his part, Whittingham said of Sunday Silence, "I just hope he didn't hurt his foot banging on my noggin that way."

Rains continued throughout the day and into Belmont eve until just past midnight. When the clouds parted, Joe King, the New York Racing Association's track superintendent, put his fifteen-man crew to work in an effort to dry the track for the Belmont Stakes program. Horsemen had been warned the previous afternoon that the main track would be closed for training on Belmont morning while the maintenance crew worked the surface over.

Saturday morning dawned sunny and breezy as the tractors continued to harrow and grade the track, whose nickname, "big sandy," suggested it would dry quickly. It did. By post time, the track was fast.

Almost as shocking as the emergence of a fast track was the fact Easy Goer, for the first time in his career, was not the betting favorite. Coupled with stablemate Awe Inspiring and in front of a hometown crowd, the Phipps entry was only the second choice in the wagering at odds of 8-5. Fans made Sunday Silence the 9-10 favorite.

Seven other three-years-old were entered. Only one of them, Imbibe, who had skipped the first two legs of the Triple Crown but was coming off a good-looking win in the Peter Pan Stakes at Belmont, was less than odds of 20-1. Imbibe, ridden by veteran Angel Cordero Jr., was 6-1 in the betting.

One of the long shots was Le Voyageur, who traveled across the Atlantic Ocean from France to contest the Belmont for owners Calumet Farm and Betty Marcus. Trained by France's Patrick Biancone, Le Voyageur was a son of 1977 Triple Crown winner Seattle Slew and produced by the champion filly, Davona Dale, who had won a series of races in New York commonly called the Filly Triple Crown. But while Le Voyageur was heavy on pedigree, he was light on experience, having raced only six times in Europe

and never on dirt. He was sent out at 29-1.

Strategy is integral to any horse race, but even more so in races that require a combination of speed and stamina to win. With only a handful of races run at a mile and a half in the United States, jockeys obviously do not have many opportunities to ride at the distance. Having a good sense of pace and knowing where to place the horse during the race are essential. Spectacular Bid's defeat in 1979 was a perfect example of a jockey having no idea when to step on the accelerator. Franklin moved his horse far too early in the race and was not able to sustain his speed to the wire.

Conversely, some will argue that the Belmont Stakes allows racing luck and strategy to come into play less than in the Derby and Preakness. Because of the configuration of the Belmont racetrack — a mile and a half in circumference and with wide, sweeping turns — fewer traffic jams transpire in the Belmont than in the Triple Crown's first two legs, and, thus, fewer excuses in defeat.

The race is billed as the "test of the champion," but it doesn't always go to the best horse. The distance of the Belmont has stopped a number of very good horses from winning the Triple Crown. Perhaps foremost among those is Northern Dancer, who set a track record winning the 1964 Kentucky Derby, a mark broken nine years later by Triple Crown winner Secretariat. Northern Dancer also won the Preakness, but the son of Nearctic couldn't stay the distance of the Belmont, finishing third behind Quadrangle.

The compact Canadian-bred colt went on to be one of the most influential sires of the second half of the twentieth century. Northern Dancer's trainer, Horatio Luro, at the age of eighty-eight, paid a visit to Whittingham, his former assistant, during Belmont week of 1989. Luro told Whittingham he liked Sunday Silence's chances of winning the Triple Crown far more than he did Northern Dancer's twenty-five years earlier.

But Luro and Whittingham were wrong, and so were those in the crowd of 64,959 who at last made Sunday Silence the favorite over Easy Goer. The Belmont Stakes, and the Triple Crown, were not to be for the sleek black son of Halo.

Le Voyageur sprinted to the early lead from the number eight post position, clicking off succeeding quarter-mile fractions of :23 1/5, :47 flat, and 1:11 1/5 for the

first three-fourths of a mile. Sunday Silence, breaking from post six, was close behind and moving easily, looking as though he could pounce on the leader at the push of a button from jockey Patrick Valenzuela. Easy Goer, in between those rivals in the starting gate in post seven, broke well, and Pat Day kept him within striking distance, well off the rail most of the way and never more than a length or two behind Sunday Silence.

The French colt continued to lead through a mile in 1:35 4/5, but Valenzuela began to ask Sunday Silence for more. The colt responded and moved quickly to the outside flank of Le Voyageur. But Easy Goer was kicking into high gear, too, and with a quarter-mile to run he powered his way past Sunday Silence in a flash. This was the Easy Goer New York fans remembered from 1988 and the spring of 1989.

Sunday Silence struggled to pass Le Voyageur in the stretch, gaining second by a length. But Easy Goer, who was four and one-half lengths clear at the eighth pole, won the Belmont by a widening eight lengths. His time of 2:26 was the second fastest in the race's long history.

"He may have run the race of his life today," Easy

Goer's trainer said.

Whittingham made no excuses for Sunday Silence. "He ran his race, but he might not want to go that far," he told reporters afterwards. "His dam was a good miler, while Easy Goer's dam was a stayer. Top-class, too. But there's nothing wrong with being a good mile to mile and quarter horse. Everybody says they make the best sires."

Sunday Silence did earn the million-dollar bonus, edging Easy Goer in Triple Crown points and easing the pain of defeat for his three owners.

The New York newspapers had fun with the reversal of fortunes. The front page of the *New York Post* carried a big, bold headline that read "LAST LAUGH! Easy Goer puts Triple Crown on arch-rival Sunday Silence." The tabloid's back page had another large-type headline saying "EASY DOES IT!"

That night McGaughey stopped by the nearby Garden City Hotel, where Whittingham was staying. The two men sat down for a drink in the lobby bar, but when it was time for Whittingham to join a group going to dinner he waved them on, ordering another round for himself and McGaughey.

A couple of hours later when the dinner party

returned to the hotel, the two Triple Crown rivals hadn't moved. They were becoming fast friends, and they regaled each other with stories until well past midnight.

"I was pretty much in awe, sitting there and swapping stories with him," McGaughey recalled. "I was just a kid going up against a legend."

Whittingham and McGaughey would have an opportunity to see each other again later in the year.

SUNDAY SILENCE

CHAPTER 10

Who's Best?

With only a few winks of sleep the night of the Belmont Stakes, Charlie Whittingham did exactly as he had done nearly every morning of his working life, rain or shine, win or lose. He arose early and got to the track before dawn.

In the stable area of Belmont Park, reporters gathered around Whittingham, many of them hoping to peel away the hard-skinned exterior of a man who, on the verge of his greatest career victory, instead had to swallow the humble pie of defeat. Whittingham would have none of it. Rather than dwell on the loss, he spun tales from his past, of other races won and lost, of favorite horses and old pals who provided a colorful landscape to this racing legend's life at the track.

One reporter asked Whittingham about how he managed to cope with the pressure he must have felt throughout the Triple Crown campaign. *Daily Racing Form* executive columnist Joe Hirsch detailed the Bald Eagle's response: "Pressure?" Whittingham asked. "The Triple Crown wasn't pressure. Pressure was when twelve of us were living in High Pockets Kelly's hotel room near San Francisco fifty years ago and none of us had enough money to contribute toward the rent. That was pressure."

With the Triple Crown now complete, both Whittingham and Easy Goer's trainer, Shug McGaughey, started looking at the next big target, the Breeders' Cup Classic, scheduled for November 4 at Gulfstream Park near Miami. Sunday Silence returned to his California base for a short rest, while Easy Goer remained at Belmont Park, where he got a brief freshening before launching a late-summer assault at Saratoga.

Perhaps Sunday Silence's rest was not long enough. Exercise rider Pam Mabes said the colt "acted like he didn't want to train" after the Triple Crown. "Normally he was so enthusiastic, but he acted like, 'No, I don't want to do this.' Charlie chalked it up to being a little tired, maybe a little overtrained."

Mabes had been concerned going into the Belmont that Sunday Silence was not at the top of his game, either. "He didn't handle that hot and muggy weather," she said. "He'd come back from galloping and hyperventilate. There was a definite change for him in New York. He didn't have the same joie de vivre."

Whittingham thought the July 23 Swaps Stakes at Hollywood Park would be easy pickings, despite the signals Sunday Silence appeared to be sending. The Swaps, run at a mile and a quarter, came six weeks after the Belmont Stakes. It was the same event that ended Triple Crown winner Seattle Slew's unbeaten record in 1977 when his owners insisted on running him over the protests of his trainer. Seattle Slew lost in a shocker, finishing fourth to J.O. Tobin and acting like a tired horse.

Prize money in the Swaps was doubled, from $200,000 to $400,000 in an effort to attract Sunday Silence. The conditions of the race called for the higher purse if a Triple Crown race winner was entered. Only four other three-year-olds signed up to take on Sunday Silence, none of which appeared to be a serious threat. Sunday Silence was sent off a 1-5 favorite by the 26,215 on hand at Hollywood Park. Second choice at 5-1 was a Florida-bred colt named Prized, who was trained by one of Whittingham's former assistants, Neil Drysdale. Prized had just one stakes victory in his career, that coming in a minor stakes at Santa Anita in March. In the Swaps, Prized carried 120 pounds, six pounds fewer than Sunday Silence. By comparison, in the Triple Crown races, all starters carried the same 126 pounds.

With a lack of early speed in the line-up, Patrick Valenzuela sent Sunday Silence to the lead, and the black colt cruised through moderate fractions of :23 3/5 for the opening quarter-mile, :47 3/5 to the half, 1:11 4/5 for six furlongs, and 1:36 2/5 for a mile. Sunday Silence looked to have the field at his mercy, with a two and one-half length advantage after a mile and a four-length lead with just a furlong to run.

Suddenly, Sunday Silence lost his momentum when he shied at the tracks left by the starting gate in mid-stretch. Prized was bearing down on the front-runner and a frantic Valenzuela smacked Sunday Silence five times on the right shoulder. His efforts had no effect. Jockey Eddie Delahoussaye, aboard Prized, said he saw

Sunday Silence weaving and shortening his stride. "He just folded it in at the eighth pole," Delahoussaye told *The Blood-Horse*, "and I knew we'd catch him."

Prized got up in the final sixteenth of a mile to win by three-quarters of a length, completing the ten furlongs in 2:01 4/5 on a fast track. Though not quite as shocking as Seattle Slew's defeat in the Swaps twelve years earlier, the defeat was a stunner.

"He wasn't loafing and waiting for other horses, he just got tired," Valenzuela was quoted as saying.

Whittingham exploded after the race, *The Blood-Horse* reported, criticizing Valenzuela for his ride. "What the hell do you have to open up five lengths for?" he snapped. "All he had to do was sit a little longer. He used a little bad judgment."

Though he blamed his jockey for the Swaps defeat, Whittingham also concluded that Sunday Silence needed more time off. He regrouped, plotting a strategy that would get him to the Breeders' Cup with a fresh and fit racehorse.

While Sunday Silence's loss was fodder to the East Coast doubters who were convinced that Easy Goer was the better horse, the Belmont Stakes winner was fortifying his own cause with a string of brilliant victories in New York.

First came a triumph over five older opponents in the Whitney Handicap at Saratoga, a nine-furlong event run at the upstate New York track on August 5. Pat Day managed to get Easy Goer into some traffic trouble around the far turn, steadying the colt on the inside as the leaders started to tire. But when Day cracked the whip on Easy Goer once they had clear sailing, the black and red Phipps colors were a blur. Easy Goer charged between horses with an explosive burst, quickly drawing off to win by four and a half lengths as a 3-10 favorite.

Two weeks after the Whitney, Easy Goer was favored over five other three-year-olds in the Travers Stakes, a mile and one-quarter event that carried a one-million-dollar purse. Known as the Mid-Summer Derby, the Travers is widely perceived as the most important race for three-year-olds outside of the Triple Crown events.

The Phipps runner was the 1-5 favorite to win the Travers. Clever Trevor, the Oklahoma-bred who showed brief speed before finishing thirteenth in the

Kentucky Derby, was the second choice. The French import Le Voyageur, the Belmont third-place finisher, was the 8-1 third choice.

As expected, Clever Trevor set the early fractions, and Easy Goer did all the late running. He drew off by three lengths, winning under a hand ride from Day and putting himself, in the eyes of many fans, back atop the three-year-old division. One of those who believed the Travers winner was the best horse in training was Saratoga's track announcer, Marshall Cassidy. As the horses approached the wire, Cassidy called out: "It's New York's Horse of the Year, Eaaaaaaasy Goer!"

After the Travers, it was back to Belmont Park for Easy Goer, who again handled older opponents with ease in the Woodward Handicap on September 16. Under the assigned weights of the race, Easy Goer carried 122 pounds, conceding between two and thirteen pounds to his opponents, plus another five pounds, theoretically, under the scale of weights that provide a five-pound weight break for three-year-olds at that time of year. The son of Alydar again won under a hand ride from Day.

With limited opportunities for three-year-olds in California following the Swaps, Whittingham decided to send Sunday Silence to the million-dollar Super Derby, a mile and one-quarter race run September 24 at Louisiana Downs near Shreveport.

Earlier that summer, Edward DeBartolo, the track's owner, tried to entice both Sunday Silence and Easy Goer to come to Louisiana, offering a two-million-dollar purse if both horses ran. McGaughey briefly considered the challenge, nominating Easy Goer to the Super Derby, but kept his star colt in New York. Instead, he sent Easy Goer's stablemate, Awe Inspiring, who was coming off a victory in the American Derby at Arlington Park in August.

Easy Goer was nearly 1,500 miles away, but he cast a very long shadow. When someone mentioned to Whittingham that his colt might be out of the running for consideration as Horse of the Year, he was quick to snap at the East Coast press. "Hell, those New Yorkers still don't think Easy Goer got beat in the Derby and Preakness," he told *Sports Illustrated*. "They aren't sure. They probably keep running them tapes over and over again."

Sunday Silence had not raced since his debacle in

the Swaps two months earlier, but he was training as enthusiastically as ever as the Super Derby approached. Two weeks before the race, in a workout at Del Mar racetrack near San Diego, Sunday Silence blazed a mile in 1:33 2/5. Only three days before the Super Derby the colt worked a quick five furlongs in :59 4/5 over the Louisiana Downs strip.

Fans also were confident that the black son of Halo was ready for a big effort, betting him down to 2-5 odds despite his defeat in the Swaps Stakes.

Awe Inspiring was Sunday Silence's principal foe, at 7-2 odds. The field of eight also included a hometown favorite, Big Earl, a Louisiana-bred gelding who had won the Prelude Stakes, the local prep race for the Super Derby. But even the locals didn't give Big Earl much of a chance, sending him off at 21-1.

When Sunday Silence left the Louisiana Downs paddock, he was wearing a new piece of equipment, a fuzzy, green shadow roll wrapped around the front of his face, a few inches above the nose. A shadow roll is designed to keep a horse's eyes from wandering too much by blocking his downward vision. In the Swaps, Sunday Silence was distracted by the tracks left by the starting gate.

He had no such problem in the Super Derby. After rating several lengths off the pace in the opening stages, a smooth-striding Sunday Silence surged to the lead around the final turn, drawing off by as many as ten lengths inside the final eighth of a mile. Valenzuela geared down on the colt in the final yards and Sunday Silence reached the wire six lengths in front. Following successive quarter-mile fractions of :23, :47 1/5, 1:12 1/5, and 1:37 4/5, he completed the ten furlongs on a fast track in 2:03 1/5. His jockey never had to uncock his whip.

The race for the runner-up spot provided an interesting sub-plot. After leading for the first half-mile, Big Earl fell back to fourth and seemed to be heading the wrong way. He dug in down the stretch, however, re-rallying to edge Awe Inspiring and another rival, Dispersal, to win a three-horse photo for second place.

Whittingham never stopped believing in Sunday Silence, but after the Super Derby his confidence level soared. "I think Sunday Silence can beat any horse running if things go his way," he told *Sports Illustrated*. "He's as good as Easy Goer. As good a horse as I've got, maybe the best I've ever had. And I've had a lot of good ones."

McGaughey, who saddled Awe Inspiring in the race, also was impressed. "Looks like I'd better have Easy Goer right on Breeders' Cup Day," he told *Sports Illustrated*. "If both horses get there the right way, it's going to be quite a race."

The Super Derby would be Sunday Silence's final race before the season-ending Breeders' Cup. McGaughey decided to give Easy Goer one final start in the million-dollar Jockey Club Gold Cup, a mile and one-half race run October 7, a month before the Breeders' Cup. Easy Goer had beaten most of his six Gold Cup opponents in either the Whitney or Woodward, but there was one new shooter in the race, Prized, who had followed up his upset of Sunday Silence in the Swaps with a triumph in the Molson Export Million Stakes at Canada's Woodbine racecourse.

Easy Goer was the 1-10 favorite, with Prized second choice at 9-2. Easy Goer won easily, moving to the lead before a mile and reaching the finish four lengths in front with little urging from his jockey. Prized was never a factor, finishing third.

The Gold Cup was the fifth successive victory in grade I races for Easy Goer since his narrow defeat in the

Preakness. It was on to Gulfstream Park and a match-up in the Breeders' Cup Classic. It was not just the three million in prize money that was at stake in the richest race of the year: the Classic would confirm either Sunday Silence or Easy Goer as Horse of the Year.

CHAPTER 11

"Much The best"

J ockey Patrick Valenzuela was a natural in the saddle, long before he launched his professional riding career as a sixteen-year-old in November of 1978 at New Mexico's Sunland Park. The native of Montrose, Colorado, was born into a family of jockeys, and there was never any doubt in his mind about what he wanted to do in life. His father, A.C. Valenzuela, was a jockey. So were four uncles, Milo, Angel, Santiago, and Mario. Angel rode once in the Kentucky Derby, finishing last of thirteen runners aboard longshot Henrijan. Milo scored in the Derby in the first of his eight rides in the race, winning with Tim Tam in 1958.

Patrick was on horseback at a very young age and made the rounds at Southern California racetracks with his father, dreaming of riding horses in big races when most kids are learning to ride a bicycle.

"When I was seven, I'd get up on Saturday mornings and go to the track and I'd be walking down the shed rows and here'd come Bill Shoemaker," Valenzuela told *The Blood-Horse*. "My dad would tell me to 'squat down and show Mr. Shoemaker how you're gonna ride when you get older.' And I'd squat down and act like I was riding."

Ten years later, he was competing with Shoemaker and other top riders, making a big name for himself as the hottest apprentice jockey to hit town in many years. After being the leading apprentice at Hollywood Park in 1979, Valenzuela set a Santa Anita record during the 1979-80 meeting for most wins by an apprentice. Trainers began to trust him with their best horses, among them D. Wayne Lukas, who gave Valenzuela the mount on Codex, winner of the 1980 Santa Anita and Hollywood derbies. By year's end, Valenzuela's mounts had earned $4,575,594, with his ten percent share giving the eighteen-year-old income of several hundred thousand dollars.

At first, Valenzuela was known as an outstanding "gate" jockey who managed to get many of his mounts to pop from the starting gate before anyone else, then get them to coast along on the lead. But he developed all-around riding skills needed for horses that came from off the pace, too. He possessed what all the great riders develop: an ability to communicate with a horse. He also had an engaging personality and a million-dollar smile.

What Valenzuela lacked was discipline. Money from his early successes was spent on fast cars and an even faster lifestyle that eventually included drugs. He was a "no-show" on countless occasions, infuriating owners and trainers who had to scramble at the last minute to replace him. But every time he came back to the racetrack, he was welcomed with open arms and an afternoon full of live mounts. His fellow riders weren't always so happy to see him. Some worried that Valenzuela might come to the jocks' room strung out on drugs, making a very dangerous occupation even more treacherous.

Valenzuela finished first with Fran's Valentine in the second Breeders' Cup race ever run, the Juvenile Fillies at Hollywood Park in 1984. Stewards disqualified her for interference at the top of the stretch after Valenzuela swerved the filly out for a clear stretch run.

Two years later, a twenty-four-year-old Valenzuela won the same race with Brave Raj, then captured the Sprint the following year with Very Subtle, both for trainer Mel Stute, who stuck with the talented rider through thick and thin.

Following his victories aboard Sunday Silence in the Kentucky Derby and Preakness Stakes, Valenzuela used his time on national television to urge kids "throughout America and the world to say 'no' to drugs." Only one year earlier on Derby day, Valenzuela was launching a comeback in New Mexico after serving a drug-related suspension. He returned to the Los Angeles area during the Oak Tree meeting in the fall of 1988, just in time to pick up the mount from Charlie Whittingham on Sunday Silence. Valenzuela wound up Oak Tree's leading rider.

Unfortunately, Valenzuela couldn't stay straight, despite having counseling for his substance-abuse problems. In late October of 1989, just one week before he was to ride Sunday Silence in the Breeders' Cup Classic and shortly after celebrating his twenty-seventh birthday, he tested positive for cocaine and was handed a sixty-day suspension. As a result,

Valenzuela lost the mount on Sunday Silence in the Breeders' Cup and a chance to earn ten percent of the winner's share of $1,350,000.

"I took off some of the biggest races in the world for a little white powder," he told *The Blood-Horse* some years later. "I didn't give myself a fair shake and I didn't give the horsemen a fair shake."

Whittingham quickly picked up the services of Chris McCarron, a California-based rider who had won the previous year's Classic with Alysheba, the Kentucky Derby and Preakness winner of 1987. "Chris is equally good, and I don't think it will make that much difference," Whittingham said. McCarron was to have ridden Mi Selecto, a long shot in the Classic, but switching to Sunday Silence was a no brainer. "I wish I could have gotten this mount under better circumstances," McCarron said. "I'm happy to be here and I wish all the best to Pat Valenzuela. He's a good friend, a good kid, and I wish nothing but the best for him."

McCarron had never ridden Sunday Silence in a race, but that week he had a chance to work the colt. The jockey likened Sunday Silence's movement to that of the two-time Horse of the Year of the early 1980s, John

Henry, whom McCarron had ridden on numerous occasions. "Unless I am really concentrating on his stride, or look down, I don't know when he changes leads," McCarron told *The Blood-Horse* after the workout.

The sixth annual running of the Breeders' Cup races were being held at South Florida's Gulfstream Park for the first time. Sunday Silence had never raced in Florida, while Gulfstream had been Easy Goer's winter home earlier in the year, when he made his 1989 debut in the Swale Stakes. But familiarity with the surroundings did not give much of a home-field advantage to the Phipps family runner. Gulfstream Park, like Santa Anita, Churchill Downs, Pimlico, and Louisiana Downs, was a one-mile oval with relatively tight turns. It was the kind of track on which Sunday Silence excelled. Easy Goer, on the other hand, had done his most effective running at Belmont Park, a mile and one-half oval with wide, sweeping turns, or the one and one-eighth miles of Saratoga.

Sunday Silence was nimble. As one of Whittingham's assistant trainers said, he could "switch leads on a dime." That agility allowed Sunday Silence to accelerate around a turn, giving him a big advantage over big, long-striding horses like Easy Goer. On long straightaways, Easy Goer had devastating power, but he didn't possess instant acceleration or an ability to accelerate around a turn. That worked to his disadvantage in the Kentucky Derby and Preakness.

One reason for Easy Goer's deficiency on tighter-turned racetracks was his puffy ankles, something trainer Shug McGaughey had to keep a close watch on throughout the chestnut's career. By the end of 1989, with ten races under him for the year, those ankles were becoming a bigger concern. The fact did not go unnoticed in the Sunday Silence camp.

"We watched the work they had to do with those ankles every day and started to really like our chances," exercise rider Pam Mabes recalled. Whittingham's confidence was building, too. "My colt will win," Whittingham told *Sports Illustrated*. "He's fresher than Easy Goer, he's quicker, and I know from experience that the longer races are harder on a horse than the shorter ones. Easy Goer just had a long one. You don't get over them so easy."

But not everyone shared that confidence. One of the doubters was Andrew Beyer, the racing columnist

for the *Washington Post* and the creator of Beyer Speed Figures, which boil down a horse's performance to a single number and allow handicappers to easily compare one horse to another. Saying Sunday Silence "has regressed" since winning the first two races of the Triple Crown, Beyer cited his speed figures to endorse Easy Goer in the Classic. The Beyer Speed Figures for Sunday Silence were 113 for the Preakness, 113 for the Belmont, 107 for the Swaps, and 106 for the Super Derby. Easy Goer's figures increased from the 113 he received in the Preakness, to 123 for the Belmont, 119 for the Whitney, 121 for the Travers, 115 for the Woodward, and 120 for the Jockey Club Gold Cup.

Easy Goer had his skeptics, too, including trainer D. Wayne Lukas, who tried to beat both horses earlier in the year with Houston and now had long shot Slew City Slew in the Classic. "I like the idea that Sunday Silence is coming off an easy win at a mile and a quarter and going to another mile and a quarter, whereas the other horse is backing up from a mile and a half," said Lukas. "And I like Charlie. I like Shug and Charlie both, but I think Charlie is the master at bringing a horse up to a classic race."

Most days, Sunday Silence was sent out to train as soon as the Gulfstream track opened, while Easy Goer went out after the track was harrowed during a break. On November 4, the morning of the Breeders' Cup, though, the track would close early, forcing McGaughey to put Easy Goer on a different training schedule.

Mabes was sitting on Sunday Silence, waiting for the gate to the track to be opened when, out of the corner of her eye, she saw a big, robust chestnut colt walking toward her. It was Easy Goer.

"Oh, my God," she said, "We're going out to train at the same time."

When the gates swung open, Mabes jogged Sunday Silence onto the Gulfstream Park surface alongside a pony, and soon thereafter was turned loose. Not far behind her was Easy Goer, with exercise rider David Carroll aboard. The two horses were only a few lengths apart as they galloped around the far turn and into the stretch. "I looked over my left shoulder and could hear someone coming up on me," Mabes recalled. "Around the eighth pole, we were going head and head."

Sunday Silence's rider looked over with a big smile on her face. "Wanna race?" she asked Carroll.

The two horses galloped together down the stretch, around the clubhouse turn, and into the backstretch. Whittingham had told Mabes to let Sunday Silence finish his gallop with a brisk three-eighths of a mile breeze, and when they reached the backstretch she asked the colt for more speed. Just then, the balmy ocean breezes picked up, and the nylon windbreaker Mabes was wearing snapped in the wind. "It was such an unbelievable moment," Mabes said. "When Easy Goer heard that sound and saw Sunday Silence take off, you could tell that he wanted to run with us. I almost took Easy Goer with me."

Carroll managed to restrain Easy Goer, allowing Sunday Silence to go ahead and finish his work. Both horses left the track and returned to their barns, awaiting the title match that would take place nearly twelve hours later in the twilight of a warm South Florida afternoon.

Breeders' Cup day started out well for McGaughey, who won the first Breeders' Cup race, the Sprint, with a 16-1 long shot named Dancing Spree, who was owned by Ogden Phipps.

When McGaughey walked back to his barn follow-

ing the winner's circle ceremonies and a round of interviews with the press, veterinarian Mark Cheney pulled
the trainer aside. Cheney, with a look on his face that
spelled trouble, told McGaughey there had been a problem with Easy Goer. "He's okay now," the veterinarian
assured, "but he colicked a little while ago."

That was anything but good news for McGaughey,
who was feeling the stress from this Horse of the Year
contest. "Doc said there was no reason not to run him,
that he seemed fine," McGaughey said.

Pat Day could feel the pressure, too. "In all my years
of riding, I have never been in a race where there was
so much riding on the outcome," Day was quoted as
saying.

A little over an hour before the Classic, McGaughey
won a second Breeders' Cup race, the Juvenile, with
Dinny Phipps' Rhythm. The momentum and karma
were definitely tipping toward Easy Goer's side until
Prized, the colt who had beaten Sunday Silence in the
Swaps Stakes, pulled off an upset in the Turf. Trainer
Neil Drysdale opted to run Prized in the mile and one-
half grass race — Prized's first race on turf — instead of
hooking up with Easy Goer and Sunday Silence in the

Classic. It was a shrewd move by Drysdale, and the victory by Prized legitimized his win over Sunday Silence in the Swaps.

Nevertheless, fans voted for Easy Goer by way of the betting windows, hammering the Alydar colt down to 1-2 odds. Sunday Silence, despite beating Easy Goer in two of their three previous meetings, was the 2-1 second choice. The six other starters seemed like little more than bit players, though it was, in fact, an accomplished group of runners. Among them was Blushing John, a colt who had begun his racing career in Europe but won several big races in the United States in 1989, including the Hollywood Gold Cup and Pimlico Special. Another was Cryptoclearance, a five-year-old with more than $3,000,000 in earnings and whose biggest victories, the Florida Derby and Donn Handicap, had come at Gulfstream Park. Western Playboy, who had run so badly against Sunday Silence, had regained his best form and was coming off a whopping seventeen-length win in the Pennsylvania Derby, albeit over easier rivals.

Present Value, like Sunday Silence a son of Halo, entered the Classic off back-to-back wins at Santa

Anita, though the competition was not nearly as stiff as he would encounter in the Breeders' Cup. The five-year-old veteran already had sixteen starts on the year, winning seven of them, but none in grade I company.

Slew City Slew was another five-year-old with plenty of experience, having raced forty-one times, with eleven wins and more than $1,000,000 in earnings. A 58-1 longshot in the betting, the best hope for the son of Seattle Slew was to go to the front at the start and try to get brave on the lead, something he hadn't done since winning the Oaklawn Handicap in April. Rounding out the field was Mi Selecto, a Canadian-based colt who pulled off an upset in his previous start, the Meadowlands Cup Handicap, a grade I race at a mile and a quarter that was his biggest career win yet. When Chris McCarron took off this 45-1 long shot, trainer Gil Rountree secured the services of Laffit Pincay Jr.

Darkness was quickly descending on Gulfstream Park when the eight runners in the Classic left the paddock and stepped onto a main track that had received some rain earlier in the day. Sunday Silence was slick with sweat and on his toes during the post parade and warm-ups. Easy Goer appeared more relaxed as he walked into the inside stall of the starting gate located in the chute at the top of the Gulfstream Park stretch. When Sunday Silence entered the number eight stall on the outside, a great roar went up from the crowd of 51,342. Dick Enberg, the NBC commentator hosting the network's marathon telecast, said the atmosphere "had the feeling of a great heavyweight fight." The broadcast team also included Tom Hammond, who termed the Classic "the race of the decade."

When the starting gates opened, Easy Goer broke a step slowly, and Day had to fight with the colt as he tried to duck toward his left as the field left the chute and entered the main track. Sunday Silence broke well and settled quickly into his steady stride, allowing the quick but fainthearted Slew City Slew to dash to the front.

Past the wire for the first time, Slew City Slew had opened up two and one-half lengths, with Blushing John second, followed along the inside by Present Value. Sunday Silence was just to Present Value's outside, about five lengths behind the leader. Easy Goer, racing in sixth position, had fallen farther back than expected, more than ten lengths from the leader.

Slew City Slew set quick fractions of :22 2/5 for the quarter-mile and :46 1/5 for the half. Midway down the backstretch, Sunday Silence crept closer to Slew City Slew, but making a more dramatic move was Easy Goer, whose long strides carried him right alongside the saddle towel of Sunday Silence.

Announcer Tom Durkin, who calls all of the Breeders' Cup races, had his eye on both horses as they made their way toward the far turn after six furlongs had been clipped off in 1:10 2/5. "Sunday Silence is bracing for the oncoming power of Easy Goer, who's right at his neck," Durkin exclaimed, "and the stage is set with three furlongs to run in the Classic."

McCarron had seen enough of Sunday Silence's races to know that he had a big advantage once his mount reached the far turn. Just as quickly as Easy Goer had pulled alongside Sunday Silence, Whittingham's charge left Easy Goer behind with a sudden burst of speed from the three-eighths pole to the top of the stretch. By then, Slew City Slew had thrown in the towel, and Blushing John and veteran jockey Angel Cordero Jr. had inherited the lead, holding a length and one-half advantage with a quarter-

mile to run. Time for the mile was 1:35 flat.

Day was whipping and driving on Easy Goer around the turn, first with the left hand, then with the right, while McCarron hadn't uncocked his stick yet. When he set Sunday Silence down at the top of the stretch, McCarron had dead aim on Blushing John and a four-length advantage on Easy Goer. He got the best of Blushing John just inside the eighth pole and set sail for home, with McCarron only waving the stick in front of Sunday Silence's eye with his left hand. Easy Goer reached his best stride in the final furlong and was bearing down quickly.

"Easy Goer set down and put to a fierce drive," Durkin called. "Sunday Silence surges to the front...Easy Goer with one final acceleration...and Sunday Silence holds on and wins by a desperate neck. Easy Goer was too late, not enough to win it, and it was Sunday Silence in a racing epic."

Arthur Hancock, watching the Classic from the box seats near the finish line, was silently transfixed on the two rivals as they began their stretch run. Staci Hancock was jumping up and down wildly, shouting "Go! Go! Go!" Arthur Hancock's good friend, bloodstock agent John Adger, was alongside, pounding him on the shoulder. "Come onnnnn," he shouted, looking frantically for the finish line in the darkness.

Arthur Hancock slowly sank to his knees, clasping his hands together in a prayerful pose. The colt that had saved his farm, brought him respect, and taken him on the racing ride of a lifetime had done it. He'd beaten Easy Goer for the third time in four meetings and clinched Eclipse Awards as champion three-year-old and, more important, Horse of the Year.

The official margin was a neck, with Easy Goer one-length clear of Blushing John, a stubborn third. Time of the race was 2:00 1/5 for the mile and one-quarter over a fast track.

Day said the incident after the start "wasn't dramatic" but that it cost Easy Goer the position he had hoped to get. The rider was happy with his position down the backstretch when he was closely pursuing Sunday Silence. "When Sunday Silence started moving at the three-eighths pole," Day said, "I wanted to go with him, and my horse was just a little slow getting started."

In the darkness of the winner's circle, NBC's Hammond asked Whittingham why he was so confident going into the Classic. "I'm an optimist," he replied. "If you're a pessimist you're not going to get very far, partner."

The Sunday Silence-Easy Goer rivalry electrified the racing world throughout 1989, and the best part for fans was that both horses would continue racing as four-year-olds.

Whittingham, the old master, got his best results from horses as they matured, and the thought of an even better version of Sunday Silence in 1990 was an exciting thought. "He's much the best horse I've trained," Whittingham said. "He's done more than any horse I've ever trained — and he isn't through yet. He's just getting going."

CHAPTER 12

Sayonara Sunday

B en Jones, the legendary horse trainer who worked for the famed Calumet Farm from the 1930s through the 1950s, once said there were only two kinds of horses: "Those that have something wrong with them and those fixin' to get something wrong with them."

During most of his two- and three-year-old season, Sunday Silence fit into the latter category. As the year wore on, however, Charlie Whittingham and veterinarian Alex Harthill became increasingly concerned with the black colt's right knee. Following his Breeders' Cup Classic victory over Easy Goer, Sunday Silence was sent back to California, where he underwent surgery on November 16 to have a small bone chip removed from that knee.

Greg Ferraro, Whittingham's attending veterinarian in California, performed the arthroscopic surgery at the

Hollywood Park Equine Clinic, with the assistance of Dr. Steve Buttgenbach. Two incisions, each measuring three-quarters of an inch long, were made on either side of the upper tripartite carpal joint, with one incision used to insert the scope and the other to remove the chip.

"There were no problems from start to finish," Ferraro told *The Blood-Horse*. "We discovered another small floating chip when we took X-rays before we went in. It was in the same joint, but on the opposite side.

"If he had to have a chip," Ferraro added, "this is the best kind to have."

Whittingham took the surgery in stride. "It's just a small chip," he said. "I've had quite a few horses that have had this. A lot race with them."

Ferraro's inspection of Sunday Silence's knee also showed some cartilage damage. "But that's to be expected under the circumstances," he said. "He will be off three or four months, but there is no reason why he shouldn't return to the races by the middle of next year."

Arthur Hancock hoped Sunday Silence would recover sufficiently to defend his title in the Breeders'

Cup. "If everything goes all right, I'd like Sunday Silence to have a shot at winning the Classic again next year," he said. "Maybe even get the earnings record. Racing needs stars, and he's certainly a popular horse."

Sunday Silence set a single-season earnings record by a North American horse when he earned $4,578,454 in 1989. The son of Halo was within shouting distance of 1988 Horse of the Year Alysheba, the all-time money winner who retired at the end of 1988 with $6,679,242 in career earnings. Only the great gelding John Henry, with $6,597,947, was between Sunday Silence and Alysheba in money won.

More important, Sunday Silence finally earned the respect he didn't get at the yearling or two-year-old in training sales, or from many fans and racing writers during his epic battles with Easy Goer. When the Horse of the Year voting was conducted, Sunday Silence was the overwhelming choice among members of the National Turf Writers Association, employees of *Daily Racing Form*, and racing secretaries at member tracks of the Thoroughbred Racing Associations of North America. Sunday Silence received 223 first-place votes to fourteen for champion older mare Bayakoa, four for

Easy Goer, and one for sprint champion Safely Kept. He also won the Eclipse Award as champion three-year-old male. Whittingham received his third Eclipse Award as outstanding trainer. Easy Goer's owner, Ogden Phipps, won his second consecutive Eclipse Award as outstanding owner.

The Horse of the Year announcement was made during a live telecast of the ABC television show *Wide World of Sports* from Santa Anita Park on January 27, 1990. Two weeks later, on February 9, at the Fontainebleau Hotel in Miami Beach, Hancock, Whittingham, and co-owner Ernest Gaillard accepted the golden statuette for Horse of the Year at the annual Eclipse Awards dinner.

While Sunday Silence was the undisputed Horse of the Year, he still had to share the spotlight with Easy Goer in what had become one of the best rivalries in the history of the sport. The Phipps family decided to keep Easy Goer in training as a four-year-old, giving racing fans the promise of more head-to-head competitions between the two colts, perhaps ending in the Breeders' Cup Classic. In 1990, the Breeders' Cup would be held at Belmont Park, where Easy Goer had the edge.

Whittingham put Sunday Silence back in training in early March, one day after he had saddled his eighth winner of the Santa Anita Handicap, better known as the Big 'Cap, the track's oldest and most prestigious race. Ruhlmann was the Big 'Cap winner, but there was no doubt in Whittingham's mind that Sunday Silence remained the "big" horse in his barn. The Bald Eagle observed how much Sunday Silence had filled out since turning four years old and was brimming with optimism about the colt's future. "From here, I can have him ready in three months," Whittingham told *The Blood-Horse* on March 5. He then repeated what he had said on the victory stand after the Breeders' Cup Classic. "He'll be a much better horse this year."

Trainer Shug McGaughey put Easy Goer back in training during the winter at Gulfstream Park, and the two men who had become friendly rivals started plotting the season ahead. With Easy Goer based in the East and Sunday Silence in the West, it was possible the two colts wouldn't meet until the fall.

There was talk of a match race between the two horses, but McGaughey pooh-poohed the idea, fearing Easy Goer would be at a major disadvantage. In most

match races, the victor is the horse who gets the early jump, and Sunday Silence possessed more early speed than Easy Goer. McGaughey wanted none of it.

Then Richard Duchossois, the energetic impresario who owned Arlington racetrack in suburban Chicago, stepped in. Duchossois had just rebuilt Arlington into a modern showplace after a devastating fire destroyed the track in 1985. Creating an event that would attract the sport's two marquee horses would give Duchossois a chance to show off his pride and joy to the racing world. He thus proposed a special invitational race, called the Arlington Challenge Cup, that would offer a million-dollar purse if both horses were in the starting line-up. If only one started, the purse would be $600,000. If neither Sunday Silence nor Easy Goer were to run, the purse would be $200,000. The Challenge Cup would be run over a mile and one-quarter on August 4 with ABC televising it live. The connections of both Sunday Silence and Easy Goer agreed to point their horses toward the special event.

Around that time, Hancock was fielding offers for Sunday Silence from an old friend, the master Japanese horseman Zenya Yoshida, that country's leading breeder. Yoshida first offered $7 million dollars to buy Sunday Silence outright, and when that offer was rejected he came back with a $10-million proposal. Terms of the deal called for Sunday Silence to complete his racing career in the United States in 1990 and then head off to stud at Yoshida's Shadai Farm on the Japanese island of Hokkaido.

"We had a nice offer, but we want to keep him here," Hancock told the *Lexington Herald-Leader*. "He's a Kentucky horse."

Yoshida knew the Hancock family quite well. In 1972, he purchased the former Hutchinson Farm in Paris, Kentucky, from a sister of Bull Hancock's and renamed it Fontainebleau Farm. Claiborne Farm was just down the road. Arthur Hancock III and Yoshida had been friends for a number of years, and one of Yoshida's sons, Teruya, had worked at Stone Farm, learning the American way of raising Thoroughbreds before he was assigned management duties at Fontainebleau. Zenya Yoshida sold the farm in the late 1980s and boarded his American-based mares at several farms, including Stone Farm.

Yoshida came back to Hancock with another offer to

buy a one-quarter interest in Sunday Silence for $2.5 million. This offer was accepted, and the Horse of the Year now was owned by a four-man partnership, each with a twenty-five percent share.

Almost to the minute, Whittingham brought Sunday Silence back to the races in the three months he said he would need. The colt's return engagement was the nine-furlong Californian Stakes at Hollywood Park on June 3. Only two other horses were willing to take on Sunday Silence, who was scheduled to be ridden again by Chris McCarron.

Earlier on that day's program, however, McCarron was involved in a frightening spill near the top of the stretch. When a horse broke down right in front of him at the five-sixteenths pole, McCarron's mount, Full Design, tripped over the fallen horse, throwing McCarron to the ground. A trailing horse stepped on the fallen jockey, breaking the thigh bone in his left leg, the fibula in his lower right leg, and the ulna in his right forearm. Four years earlier, McCarron had broken the same bone in his left leg and was out five months.

The thirty-five-year-old McCarron, who the previous year had been inducted into the National Museum

181

of Racing Hall of Fame, spent that night in nearby Centinela Hospital, where he was treated by the renowned orthopedic surgeon Dr. Robert Kerlan. The other rider involved in the spill, Kent Desormeaux, suffered a fractured rib and bruised others.

Whittingham won the race in which McCarron was injured, and in the winner's circle he was surrounded by agents for other jockeys hoping to get their riders named on Sunday Silence later that afternoon. But Whittingham decided to give another chance to Sunday Silence's former rider, Patrick Valenzuela, who had served out his suspension from the previous year and was doing his best to stay clear of drugs and alcohol.

"I pray for Chris and Kent's recovery, but I try to block those spills out of my mind," Valenzuela told *The Blood-Horse* after learning he would be reunited with Sunday Silence.

With Valenzuela back aboard, Sunday Silence won the Californian easily, going wire to wire after breaking awkwardly from the starting gate. He was the 1-10 favorite in the betting, and though the winning margin was just three-quarters of a length, Sunday Silence and Valenzuela could have won by more. Whittingham

reminded the jockey not to use the whip, and also told him not to win by too many lengths, fearing that a romping victory would encourage racing secretaries to pile heavy weight assignments on Sunday Silence in upcoming handicap races.

"He's very honest, not a hard horse to ride," Whittingham told *The Blood-Horse*. "He just don't like the stick on him. He can be ornery. Not difficult but ornery. He didn't have too tough a race, and now we've got three weeks til the next one."

The next one was the mile and one-quarter Hollywood Gold Cup, a one-million dollar handicap race on June 24. Sunday Silence was assigned the high weight of 126 pounds, five pounds more than a son of Alydar named Criminal Type, who carried the silks of Calumet Farm and was trained by D. Wayne Lukas. Early in the year, Criminal Type was a complete unknown, but he made a name for himself in late May when he defeated Easy Goer at Belmont Park in the one-mile Metropolitan Handicap. The champion sprinter Housebuster finished second in the race, with Easy Goer third, beaten a length and three-quarters.

Ruhlmann and Sunday Silence raced in the Gold

Cup as an entry for Whittingham, going off at odds of 1-2. The speedy Ruhlmann set the early fractions in the race, the half-mile in :46 4/5, six furlongs in 1:10 1/5, and a mile in 1:34 3/5. Criminal Type was in hot pursuit of the frontrunner, with Sunday Silence glued to his outside hip.

At the top of the stretch, Ruhlmann gave way, and the Gold Cup became a two-horse race between Criminal Type and Sunday Silence. They had raced as a team most of the way around the Hollywood Park oval, and went stride for stride down the stretch, with Criminal Type holding a narrow advantage throughout. Sunday Silence never could pass the Calumet runner, falling a head short at the wire. Criminal Type covered the distance in a very quick 1:59 4/5.

"I thought I had him," Valenzuela said after the race. "I never got in front of Criminal Type. I got real close to him, but that was all. The other horse got a neck in front of me and that was when I went to the whip. My horse ran a super race, but I think the five pounds made the difference."

Whittingham agreed, fuming about the weight assignments. "He (Criminal Type) picks up one pound after beating the best horses in New York," he told the Associated Press. "Joe Hirsch (the *Daily Racing Form* columnist) says five pounds means five lengths at a mile and a quarter, so there you have it. I would have liked to have been equal-weighted today. That's what got it. At equal weights, I think we would have beat him."

Easy Goer's earlier loss to Criminal Type was even more shocking than Sunday Silence's defeat. The Phipps runner was sent away the 2-5 favorite following a smashing seasonal debut in May at Belmont Park, where he won a minor stakes race, the Gold Stage, by seven and one-half lengths, going seven furlongs on a sloppy track in 1:22 1/5.

But Easy Goer came up lame after winning the Gold Stage. McGaughey trained him with bar shoes to protect his feet and later admitted that he rushed the colt, giving him just twelve days between the Gold Stage and his losing effort in the Metropolitan mile.

On July 4, Easy Goer bounced back, winning the Suburban Handicap by three and three-quarters lengths as the 1-5 favorite. He covered the mile and one-quarter on a fast track in 2:00.

Despite Sunday Silence's narrow loss to Criminal

Type, anticipation among racing fans for the Arlington Challenge Cup was at a fever pitch for the first head-to-head match between the two horses since the previous year's Breeders' Cup Classic.

Then things suddenly unraveled.

Two weeks after winning the Suburban, Easy Goer fractured a sesamoid in his foot while breezing in preparation for the Arlington race. The Phippses were in Iceland on a fishing trip, and McGaughey didn't want to tell the racing press about Easy Goer's injury until he could reach them. Once he was able to contact them, he announced the sad news that Easy Goer had been retired.

Whittingham didn't change his plans with Sunday Silence, shipping the colt to Chicago to train for a race whose purse had now been cut from one million to $600,000. Everything was going well until the Tuesday before the race, when Sunday Silence started favoring his left front leg while pulling up after a four-furlong workout. X-rays were taken of his ankle, but they did not reveal an injury.

Sunday Silence went back to the track the following day, but it was clear he was not one-hundred percent, nodding his head as he jogged. Harthill was on the scene, prescribing phenylbutazone to reduce inflammation and putting the ankle in a tub of ice. After a thorough examination on August 2 that included an ultrasound scan of the ankle, Harthill consulted with Whittingham and Sunday Silence's other owners and recommended the Horse of the Year be retired. Two weeks after his arch rival was injured, Sunday Silence had his career cut short, too.

The injury was described as a slight tear in the distal sesamoidean ligament that attaches to the sesamoids, the two small bones behind the lower part of the ankle. Commonly referred to as the XYZ ligaments, the ligaments run the length of the pastern and are an important part of the support mechanism that is critical to a horse's ability to bear weight.

"Hell, doc, that sounds like the end of the alphabet," Whittingham said to Harthill after the veterinarian described the injury to him.

"He could have gotten through the race but if we didn't, or if he got beat by some coyote, that wouldn't do him much good either, and the wolves would eat him alive," Whittingham told the *Herald-Leader*.

"If he just went along and ran he'd be fine," Harthill told the paper. "But if he got bumped or thrown off stride and had to catch himself and quickly recover, it could be disastrous."

The end came shockingly fast. As Harthill said, "The baby was born and named in one day."

"When I first heard about it, you just want to go somewhere and curl up," Hancock told the *Herald-Leader*. "It's a shame, but at least he's not in a hospital somewhere, hurt."

Arlington's Challenge Cup, once vaunted as the race of the year, was reduced to a small field of mostly forgettable horses. Racing fans felt cheated at the missed opportunity to see one last match between the robust chestnut, Easy Goer, and the sleek black running machine, Sunday Silence.

Sunday Silence's career ended with a sparkling record of nine victories and five second-place finishes from fourteen starts. He earned $4,968,554. Easy Goer won fourteen of twenty starts, with five seconds and one third, for earnings of $4,873,770. Even in money won, little separated these two great champions.

Exercise rider Pam Mabes and groom Charles Clay,

who had spent so much time with this feisty son of Halo over the previous two years, accompanied the colt on the van ride from Chicago to Stone Farm. They stayed with Sunday Silence for a week until he was acclimated to his new surroundings, then returned to Whittingham's barn in California. "It was very hard to say goodbye," said Mabes.

After the retirement, Arthur Hancock began calling breeders in an effort to syndicate Sunday Silence into forty shares at a cost of $250,000 apiece. His stud fee was set at $50,000 for each live foal. But the snubbing that Sunday Silence got early in his career reared its ugly head again. While Seth Hancock at Claiborne Farm had no trouble convincing breeders to send some of their best mares to Easy Goer for the 1991 breeding season, Arthur was getting the cold shoulder. The stud fee for Easy Goer, who was not being syndicated by owner Ogden Phipps, was twice as high as Sunday Silence's, $100,000.

"Nobody wanted him," Hancock said. "Well, there were three people — Dick Duchossois, Josephine Abercrombie, and Tom Tatham — but that was it. On top of that, nobody was calling to book to breed to him, except Warner Jones and a friend of Charlie's. Normally a horse like that will come in and we would be flooded with calls."

Hancock still had a growing family and bills to pay. "I'm needy, not greedy," he liked to say. Zenya Yoshida renewed his offer to buy Sunday Silence and stand him at his farm in Japan. In September, Hancock reluctantly agreed to sell. By late October, when most racing fans had hoped to see Sunday Silence competing with Easy Goer in the Breeders' Cup at Belmont Park, he was on his way to Japan.

"It was the most wrenching decision I've had to make," Hancock said. "If we could have gotten half the shares sold we could have swung it — just a little help, but we couldn't."

Yoshida paid over $11 million for Sunday Silence: $2.5 million for his early twenty-five percent share, $7.5 million to buy out the other three partners, plus additional compensation for four lifetime breeding rights and three-fourths of a share for Whittingham as trainer. Many so-called experts scoffed at the amount the Japanese breeder paid for a son of Halo out of a mare whose pedigree was lacking in commercial appeal.

But Yoshida got the last laugh. His purchase of Sunday Silence might have been the deal of the twentieth century.

CHAPTER 13

Best In The World

Z enya Yoshida had built a Thoroughbred breeding dynasty in Japan long before his purchase of Sunday Silence in the fall of 1990. The roots of Shadai Farm were established by his father, Zensuke Yoshida, a dairy cattleman who imported sixteen Thoroughbreds from the United States in 1928.

Born on May 3, 1921, near Sapporo, Japan, Zenya Yoshida was a horseman throughout his life, establishing his own farm in 1939 and carrying on his father's operation when he died. In the 1950s, Yoshida began flying to the United States to purchase horses himself, importing stallions and mares and buying the occasional yearling to race in America or Europe. He made a big splash in 1973 at the Keeneland July yearling sale when, as part of a syndicate, he spent a then-record price of $600,000 to buy Wajima, a colt from the last crop of champion sire Bold Ruler, a mainstay at Bull Hancock's Claiborne Farm.

Yoshida had a flair for showmanship. In 1975, when Wajima defeated Horse of the Year Forego in the $250,000 Marlboro Cup Invitational Handicap at Belmont Park, the Japanese owner showed his appreciation to the sponsor, holding up a pack of Marlboro cigarettes in the winner's circle during CBS's live telecast of the race. Wajima went on to be that year's champion three-year-old colt.

Fourteen years later, at the 1989 Keeneland July sale, Yoshida took center stage again, bidding $2.8 million to buy the last yearling by the great sire Northern Dancer ever to be offered at public auction. It was an electrifying moment when the bidding stopped. Yoshida was recognized from the auction stand and took a deep bow as the spectators in the sale pavilion offered a round of applause in appreciation of the moment.

But it was another son of Northern Dancer purchased by Yoshida from Canadian E.P. Taylor at the 1972 Saratoga yearling sale that propelled his breeding operation far ahead of the competition in his native country. Yoshida paid $100,000 for the striking chestnut colt whose face was almost entirely covered by a broad, white blaze. Named Northern Taste, the colt won a group I race in France, then retired to Shadai Farm, where he became Japan's dominant stallion. During one stretch, from 1982 to 1992, he was the nation's leading sire by progeny earnings. As Northern Taste's daughters entered the breeding shed as broodmares, he eventually became Japan's leading broodmare sire.

By the time Sunday Silence arrived late in 1990, the Shadai operation was massive, with several hundred broodmares and sixteen stallions, many of them European or American imports that had won some of the world's most important races. The quality of the broodmare band had improved significantly in the late 1980s and early 1990s. While the American bloodstock market was in a severe slump, Japanese racing and breeding were booming. The yen was strong in currency markets, giving Yoshida and other Japanese horsemen excellent buying opportunities at Thoroughbred auctions in the United States and Europe.

After purchasing Sunday Silence, Yoshida quickly syndicated the horse into sixty shares, each valued at approximately $300,000. Shadai kept half, meaning

Yoshida got $9 million for thirty shares, recouping most of his investment before Sunday Silence had been bred to his first mare.

Yoshida took advantage of the fact Sunday Silence was a complete outcross to Northern Dancer and Raise a Native — the two most popular sire lines in the world — and bred many of his Northern Taste mares to his new stallion. During Sunday Silence's initial year at stud, seasons to outside breeders were sold at a cost of 10 million Japanese yen — an amount approximately equal to $77,000 in converted funds in February 1991. From his first crop of sixty-seven foals born in 1992, fifteen were produced from mares by Northern Taste. Another twelve were from daughters of Northern Dancer or some of his other sons and grandsons, including Nijinsky II, Danzig, and Lyphard. It was clear Zenya Yoshida was determined to give Sunday Silence the best opportunity to prove himself at stud.

Unfortunately, the elder Yoshida never had the chance to see the legacy he had created. He died from heart failure on August 13, 1993, when Sunday Silence's first foals were yearlings.

That first crop produced fifty-nine runners, with

forty-seven of them winning at least one race. An amazing twelve of them, or eighteen percent of his first-year foals, became stakes winners. The racetrack earnings from this one crop exceeded $50 million.

In that first crop was Fuji Kiseki, Japan's champion two-year-old colt of 1994 and the spitting image of Sunday Silence. When his career was cut short by injury early in 1995, Fuji Kiseki became the first of many sons of Sunday Silence to enter stud.

Later that year, sons of Sunday Silence finished one-two in the Tokyo Yushun, or Japanese Derby. The winner was Tayasu Tsuyoshi, with Genuine finishing second. Teruya Yoshida stood proudly on the victory stand in the traditional Japanese ceremonies honoring the winning owner, breeder, trainer, groom, and jockey of a stakes winner. Shadai Farm bred both Tayasu Tsuyoshi and Genuine.

"Unbelievable," Yoshida said after the Derby. "It is unbelievable that both horses are just like their father. When someone comes to them, they fight back."

Also from that first crop was Dance Partner, winner of the Yushun Himba, or Japanese Oaks, one week before the Sunday Silence colts swept the Derby. Dance Partner, named champion three-year-old filly in 1995 and champion older mare in 1996, was the first son or daughter of Sunday Silence to compete in Europe, where she finished a close second in the 1995 Prix de la Nonette, a group III race at Deauville in France.

Sunday Silence sired a third champion from that first crop, Marvelous Sunday, who was named best older horse as a five-year-old in 1997.

Sunday Silence was the leader among freshman sires of 1994, and when his second crop of foals reached the races the following year, he topped Japan's general sire list for the first time. That second crop included another two-year-old male champion, Bubble Gum Fellow, plus a colt named Dance in the Dark, who was named champion three-year-old colt in 1996.

As his success and fame rose among Japanese breeders, so did Sunday Silence's stud fee. Although Japanese stud fees usually are not published, individual no-guarantee breeding seasons sold on the open market in 1995 were priced as high as twenty-million yen, approximately $235,000. That didn't slow down the demand among breeders. Sunday Silence produced 129 foals the following year, 1996, then followed with foal crops of 158 and 157 in 1997 and 1998, respectively. The annual value of Sunday Silence's stud fees began to approach fifty million.

In 2000, Sunday Silence was bred to two hundred mares, and Teruya Yoshida said the number could have been higher. "The Japanese people want the number of seasons increased," Teruya Yoshida told *The Blood-Horse*, "so more of them can buy. But that is the maximum number, even though his fertility is good."

By 2001, when his eighth crop reached racing age, Sunday Silence had 822 foals aged two or older, with 703 of them having raced, and 457 winning at least one race. Sixty-three of Sunday Silence's offspring had won a stakes, and the total progeny earnings exceeded $270 million. Fifty-six of his runners had earned more than one-million apiece. The average earnings per runner was an astounding $391,114. Sunday Silence has completely dominated the annual sire list in Japan, finishing first every year since 1995, with his offspring often earning double the amount of money won by the progeny of his closest pursuer.

In 2000, runners by Sunday Silence earned more than fifty-million dollars racing in Japan. By comparison, North America's leading sire, Storm Cat, had progeny earnings of just over nine-million in the United States and Europe.

The breeding of Sunday Silence to mares sired by Northern Taste has been tried eighty-seven times, far more than any other sire-broodmare sire cross.

"We sent our good daughters of Northern Taste to him, but he's proven to be very flexible," Teruya Yoshida told *The Blood-Horse*. "He works with just about any kind of mare. He can go with a long-distance mare or he can go with a short-distance mare."

Asuka Kumekawa, a young horsewoman who works for another of Zenya Yoshida's sons, Katsumi, owner of Northern Farm, translated comments for *The Blood-Horse* from Sunday Silence's groom, Naoki Sakota.

"He says Sunday Silence is like a breeding machine; he doesn't get depressed about work when he covers a lot of mares," Kumekawa said. "He has been with Sunday Silence a long time, and he really likes the horse. However, he would like to mention a few things. He says that Sunday Silence is very aggressive. He has had many bites from the horse. It's almost a miracle, he says, that they both have all their body parts intact."

Kumekawa then described the physical characteristics of the typical Sunday Silence foal.

"Sickle-hocked and cow-hocked, offset knees, and

sloppy pasterns," she said. "Everyone, if you don't tell them they are looking at a Sunday Silence foal, they say, 'I don't like that hock,' or 'I don't like those pasterns.' But if you tell them, 'This is a Sunday Silence foal,' they say, 'Wow!' In the Sunday Silence way, they are beautiful horses. Of all the foals on Northern Farm, they are the heaviest in terms of average birth weight. Genetically, they are fast growing, and they have good hearts, good brains, and good muscles."

Sunday Silence's popularity extends far beyond breeders in his adopted land. Despite never having raced outside of the United States, Sunday Silence has become a celebrity to Japanese racing fans because of the success of his offspring. Each spring and summer, once the harsh, snowy winters of Hokkaido have made way for the lush green pastures and pleasant temperatures, busloads of racing fans stop by Shadai Farm to see the number one stallion.

Fans can get more than souvenir snapshots of their favorite horses at Shadai or many of the other farms on Hokkaido. The Yoshidas have manufactured countless souvenirs featuring images of many of their horses, but most notably Sunday Silence. They developed an entire product line of Sunday Silence hats, shirts, jackets, sweatbands, and socks. All of the Sunday Silence merchandise is black, with no lettering, but a likeness of the distinctive thin, white blaze that runs the length of his face. The Sunday Silence blaze is as recognizable to Japanese racing fans as the Nike swoosh is to American sports fans.

Zenya Yoshida continues to watch the activity, symbolically at least, from a vantage point on a small rise near the stallion barn, where a striking statue of him is located. It serves as a reminder to visitors that it was the elder Yoshida who had the vision and confidence to build one of the largest and most successful Thoroughbred operations in the world.

In May of 1996, Shadai Farm hosted a special visitor who had traveled halfway around the world just to see Sunday Silence. "Do you remember me?" the man said, looking into the eyes of the horse that nearly died on a cold Thanksgiving Day nearly ten years earlier. History didn't record whether or not the black colt acknowledged the inquiry.

But the visitor, Arthur Hancock III, would never forget Sunday Silence. The horse was, as Hancock liked to say, "a gift from God."

EPILOGUE

Rivalry Enshrined

Ten years after he sold the 1989 Horse of the Year to Zenya Yoshida, Arthur Hancock had another Sunday Silence he was trying to peddle. This one, however, was a music CD named after the horse that saved Hancock and Stone Farm from bankruptcy. The CD, with fourteen bluegrass songs, including, of course, "Sunday Silence," was recorded by Hancock with some of country music's top studio musicians in Nashville, Tennessee.

Hancock hadn't given up on the horse business. In fact, the CD's release coincided with the 2000 Kentucky Derby triumph of a horse Hancock bred in partnership with Robert and Janice McNair's Stonerside Farm. The colt, Fusaichi Pegasus, was purchased for $4,000,000 at the 1998 Keeneland July yearling sale from the Stone Farm consignment by another Japanese owner, Fusao Sekiguchi, who raced the colt in partnership with Teruya

Yoshida. A majority interest in Fusaichi Pegasus was sold at the end of his three-year-old season for a sum that placed his overall value at approximately $70 million — an all-time record for a stallion prospect.

So, in addition to raising and co-owning the horse that became the world's biggest money-making stallion, Hancock co-bred a colt that sold for more as a stallion prospect than any other horse in history.

Sunday Silence's trainer, Charlie Whittingham, died on April 20, 1999, one week after his eighty-sixth birthday. The 1989 Horse of the Year campaign by Sunday Silence was far from being the Bald Eagle's last hurrah as a trainer. He guided the Affirmed filly Flawlessly to back-to-back Eclipse Awards in 1992 and 1993 and came close to a third Kentucky Derby triumph in 1994 when Strodes Creek finished second to Go for Gin. Whittingham also co-owned Strodes Creek with Hancock and another partner.

Tom Tatham, the breeder of Sunday Silence, continues to run a large operation with approximately thirty broodmares and calls Arthur Hancock one of his best friends. Tatham had hoped to send some mares to Japan to breed to Sunday Silence, but said the logistics made it nearly impossible to do so. He regrets letting the horse slip through his hands and said the Sunday Silence episode reminded him of one Charlie Whittingham's old sayings: "Never say anything bad about a horse until he's been dead at least fifteen years."

Ted Keefer, the adviser to Tatham who recommended getting rid of Sunday Silence, said he has no regrets about his thumbs-down appraisal. "I looked at him the way I look at every horse," Keefer said. "His physical problems weren't minor; they were major. In my opinion, Sunday Silence was a freak. With his conformation, 999 out of 1,000 horses would never have gotten to the races, let alone be a champion or a champion sire. But I have no regrets and I'm proud for everybody who did so well with him," he said.

Late in 2001, at the age of thirty-nine, jockey Patrick Valenzuela was attempting another comeback after losing his jockey's license the previous year because of continued problems with substance abuse. The 1990s had not been kind to Valenzuela, but, as the troubled rider said, "I haven't been very good to myself, either."

Sunday Silence's rival, Easy Goer, died a sudden and tragic death on May 12, 1994. Easy Goer galloped around his paddock that afternoon, staggered, then fell to the ground. He was dead in seconds. An autopsy concluded that Easy Goer died from anaphylactic shock.

The chestnut colt came to Claiborne Farm with high expectations, and was bedded down in the stall previously reserved for Triple Crown winner Secretariat, and before him by his sire, Bold Ruler. Easy Goer sired just four crops of foals, and though he was represented by grade I winners My Flag, Will's Way, and Furlough, his record as a stallion was disappointing.

Halo, Sunday Silence's sire, lived a long and productive life, succumbing to a heart attack at the age of thirty-one in November of 2000. He sired sixty-two stakes winners, but none of them came close to achieving what Sunday Silence did as a three-year-old in 1989. Halo was buried at Stone Farm.

Sunday Silence and Easy Goer went head to head for the last time in 1996, when both horses became eligible for election into the National Museum of Racing Hall of Fame. Sunday Silence got the nod over his rival and was inducted in his first year of eligibility. Easy Goer was elected into the Hall of Fame the following year.

Somehow, it's fitting that they are back together again.

		Turn-to, 1951	Royal Charger Source Sucree
	Hail to Reason, 1958	Nothirdchance, 1948	Blue Swords Galla Colors
HALO, dkb/br, 1969	Cosmah, 1953	Cosmic Bomb, 1944	Pharamond II Banish Fear
		Almahmoud, 1947	Mahmoud Arbitrator
SUNDAY SILENCE, dark bay or brown colt, 1986	Understanding, 1963	Promised Land, 1954	Palestinian Mahmoudess
		Pretty Ways, 1953	Stymie Pretty Jo
WISHING WELL, b, 1975	Mountain Flower, 1964	Montparnasse II, 1956	Gulf Stream Mignon
		Edelweiss, 1959	Hillary Dowager

SUNDAY SILENCE's RACE RECORD

Sunday Silence — **dkbbr. c. 1986, by Halo (Hail to Reason)–Wishing Well, by Understanding** — **Lifetime record: 14 9 5 0 $4,968,554**

Own.– Gaillard & Hancock III & Whittingham et al
Br.– Oak Cliff Thoroughbreds Ltd (Ky)
Tr.– Charles Whittingham

24Jun90- 8Hol	fst 1¼	:464 1:101 1:343 1:594	3↑ Hol Gold Cup H-G1	4	4	31½	2hd	2hd	2hd	Valenzuela PA	126	*.50e	98-09	CriminalType121hdSndaySilnce1263½OpnngVrs1192¾	Gamely	7
3Jun90- 9Hol	fst 1⅛	:471 1:104 1:351 1:48	3↑ Californian-G1	2	1	1½	1½	11½	1¾	Valenzuela PA	126	*.10	94-14	Sunday Silence126¾Stylish Winner1153Charlatan III111		3
Awkward break;Previously owned by Gaillard & Hancock III & Whittingham																
4Nov89-10GP	fst 1¼	:461 1:102 1:35 2:001	3↑ BC Classic-G1	8	4	35	21½	2hd	1nk	McCarron CJ	122	2.00	107-01	SndaySlnc122nkEsyGr1221BlushngJohn1269¾	Good handling	8
24Sep89-10LaD	fst 1¼	:471 1:121 1:374 2:031	Super Derby-G1	7	5	42½	1hd	14	16	Valenzuela PA	126	*.40	85-15	SundaySilence1266BigEarl126hdAweInspiring126nk	Drew out	8
23Jly89- 8Hol	fst 1¼	:473 1:114 1:362 2:014	Swaps-G2	2	1	11½	12½	14	2¾	Valenzuela PA	126	*.20	82-18	Prized120¾Sunday Silence12610Endow1231¼	Lugged out late	5
10Jun89- 8Bel	fst 1½	:47 1:111 2:004 2:26	Belmont-G1	6	3	21½	21	24½	28	Valenzuela PA	126	*.90	82-13	Easy Goer1268Sunday Silence1261Le Voyageur12612		10
Brief lead,weakened																
20May89-10Pim	fst 1 3/16	:462 1:093 1:341 1:534	Preakness-G1	7	4	33	32	1hd	1no	Valenzuela PA	126	2.10	98-10	Sunday Silence126noEasy Goer1265Rock Point1262		8
Bumped,steadied,brsh																
6May89- 8CD	my 1¼	:463 1:112 1:374 2:05	Ky Derby-G1	10	4	46½	31	11½	12½	Valenzuela PA	126	3.10	72-28	Sunday Silence1262½Easy Goer126hdAwe Inspiring126¾		15
Steadied st,swerved																
8Apr89- 5SA	fst 1⅛	:453 1:093 1:344 1:473	S A Derby-G1	4	3	32	2½	16	111	Valenzuela PA	122	2.40	91-12	Sunday Silence12211Flying Continental122¾Music Merci122½		6
Jostled start																
19Mar89- 8SA	fst 1 1/16	:221 :451 1:091 1:423	San Felipe H-G2	5	4	24	24	12	11¾	Valenzuela PA	119	2.90	88-16	SundaySilnce1191¾Flying Continental1183½Music Merci1243½		5
Broke awkwardly																
2Mar89- 7SA	sly 6½f	:213 :443 1:084 1:152	Alw 32000	5	2	1hd	11	13½	14½	Valenzuela PA	119	*.90	93-18	SndaySilnce1194½HeroicType119¾MightBRght1193½	Driving	7
3Dec88- 3Hol	fst 6½f	:22 :443 1:094 1:163	Alw 24000	1	5	31½	1½	11½	2hd	Gryder AT	120	1.80	92-12	Houston120hdSunday Silence1201¼Three Times Older1172		7
Lugged out lt																
13Nov88- 2Hol	fst 6f	:22 :444 :564 1:092	Md Sp Wt	9	2	21½	1½	14	110	Valenzuela PA	118	*.70	95-13	SundaySilnce11810Moment of Time118¾Northern Drama1181¼		10
Veered out st																
30Oct88- 6SA	fst 6½f	:214 :451 1:102 1:17	Md Sp Wt	11	7	32	2hd	11	2nk	Valenzuela PA	118	*1.50	85-13	CroLover118nkSndaySlnc1187½GrnStorm118hd	Raced greenly	12

Index

Abercrombie, Josephine 189

Adger, John 25, 51, 172

Affirmed 74, 83, 128-130, 203

Almahmoud..28, 40

Alydar...74-75, 89, 94, 121, 128-131, 151, 167, 183

Alysheba 131, 160, 176

Arlington Challenge Cup...179, 186, 188

Awe Inspiring...99, 105, 109, 138, 151-154

Belmont Park 29-31, 52, 68, 71, 75-76, 78, 119, 127, 129, 133, 136, 144
                                145, 150, 161, 177, 183, 185, 190, 193

Belmont Stakes 102, 127, 137, 139, 141, 144, 146, 149

Beyer Speed Figures 163

Blenheim II...17, 40

Blushing John 167, 169-172

Bold Ruler...17, 42-43, 73, 83, 193, 204

Brave Raj 159

Breeders' Cup Classic 9, 25, 39, 145, 155, 159, 174, 177-178, 186

Bubble Gum Fellow...197

Buckpasser 74

Buttgenbach, Dr. Steve 175

Campbell, Alex 51

Carroll, Joe 115

Cheney, Mark 166

Churchill Downs 18, 52, 61, 65, 77, 79, 82, 85, 87, 89, 95-96, 98,
                                100-101, 103-105, 114, 121, 128, 161

Claiborne Farm.......11, 17, 29, 31, 40, 42, 56, 60-61, 74, 180, 189, 193, 204

Clay, Charles...103, 117, 125, 133, 188

Codex...88, 157

Cosmah..28-29

Country Queen 36-39

Criminal Type 183-185

Cryptoclearance 167

Dance in the Dark 197

Dance Partner 196

Dansil 100, 107, 109, 122

Day, Pat 76, 90, 101, 141, 149, 166

Delahoussaye, Eddie 18, 147

Denman, Trevor 92, 124

Devil's Bag 27, 40

Divine Comedy 82

Drysdale, Neil 147, 166

Duchossois, Richard 179, 189

Easy Goer.....9, 70-71, 74-79, 89-91, 94-96, 98-101, 104-109, 112, 119-128,
130-132, 136, 138, 141-143, 145, 149-152, 154-155, 161-167, 169-172,
174, 176-179, 183, 185-186, 188-190, 204-205

Eclipse Award 73, 79, 128, 177

Ellerslie Farm 11, 14

Engelhard, Charles W. 29

Ferdinand 57, 64, 69, 82-86, 95

Ferraro, Dr. Greg 174-175

Flawlessly 203

Flying Continental 88, 91-92, 100, 109

Fontainebleau Farm 180

Forli 60

Fran's Valentine 158

Fuji Kiseki 196

Fusaichi Pegasus 202-203

Gaillard, Dr. Ernest 51, 177

Gato Del Sol 18-20, 52

Genuine 36, 196

Gone Fishin' 82

Goodbye Halo 51-55, 61, 65-66, 78, 80

Gotham Stakes 89, 94

Gryder, Aaron 65, 68-69

Gulfstream Park....................83, 89, 91, 145, 155, 161, 164, 167-169, 178

Hail to Reason 27, 31-32

Hall of Fame 26, 32, 56, 58, 64, 73, 82, 86, 93, 182, 205

Halo 6-7, 23, 27-32, 40-41, 45-48, 50-56, 61, 65-66, 78, 80, 87,
141, 152, 167, 176, 189-190, 205

Hancock, Arthur B. III.........8, 10-17, 20-21, 23, 25, 40-41, 56, 61, 75, 80,
91, 97, 109, 116, 122, 132, 134, 171-172, 175, 180, 189, 201-203

Hancock, Arthur Boyd..14

Hancock, Bull.....................................10-11, 13, 17, 31, 56, 60-61, 180, 193

Hancock, Capt. Richard Johnson 14

Hancock, Seth...12, 75, 189

Hancock, Staci 10, 20, 23, 171

Harthill, Dr. Alex.......................114-115, 120, 125, 132-133, 174, 187-188

Hawkster..90, 100, 109, 122

Hillary...33-34

Hollywood Gold Cup 167, 183

Hollywood Park..........33-34, 36-38, 49, 51, 56, 67-68, 128, 146, 157-158,
175, 181, 184

Horse of the Year....................42, 60, 73-74, 150-151, 155, 160, 166, 172,
176-177, 181, 187, 193, 202-203

Houston 24, 67-68, 90-92, 99, 105-109, 122-124, 163

Japan 9-10, 190, 192, 194, 196-198, 204

Johnson, Janet...57

Johnstown 17

Jones, Gary...32, 35, 44

Keefer, Ted 25, 43-44, 48, 56

Keeneland................18, 25, 29, 44, 46-48, 53, 67, 100, 128, 192-193, 202

Kenney, Charles..11

Kentucky Derby..9, 16-17, 19, 26-27, 31, 33-34, 36, 43, 49-50, 52-53, 57,
61, 68-69, 79-83, 85-86, 89, 91, 97, 99-100, 112-113, 120, 122, 129-131,
133, 140, 150, 156, 159-160, 162, 202-203

King, Joe...137

Kumekawa, Asuka...199

Le Voyageur 138-139, 141-142, 150

Lively One 50, 61, 87

Llangollen Farm 59-60

Louisiana Downs...151-152, 161

Lukas, D. Wayne 52, 68, 72, 99, 122, 157, 163, 183

Luro, Horatio 18, 58, 140

Mabes, Pam..............50-51, 57-58, 61-65, 96-97, 114, 117-118, 125, 137,
145, 162, 164-165, 188-189

Mahmoud 28, 40

Marvelous Sunday..197

McCarron, Chris.......................................160-161, 168, 170-171, 181-182

McGaughey, Claude R. III...71-72, 75-79, 90, 92-94, 98-99, 104, 112-113,
119, 121, 127, 136, 143, 145, 151, 154, 162, 164-166, 178-179, 185-186

Miller, Mackenzie 29

Mi Selecto 160, 168

Morrison, Carl 7

Music Merci 87-88, 90-92

Nasrullah 17, 42

Natalma 28-29

Northern Dancer...27, 29, 34, 140-141, 193, 195

Northern Farm 199-200

Northern Taste..194-195, 199

Northern Wolf 100, 102, 106-109, 122-123

Oak Cliff...24-26, 43-44, 48

Phipps, Ogden....................11-12, 42, 52, 66, 71-77, 89, 95, 99-100, 121,
123, 127, 138, 149-150, 161, 165-166, 177, 185, 189

Pimlico 113-114, 118-119, 121-122, 132, 161, 167

Pleasant Colony 18, 131

Porterhouse 60, 83

Preakness Stakes 53, 102, 111, 113, 115-117, 119-122, 124,
126, 128-131, 133, 139-140, 152, 155, 159-160, 162-163

Present Value 167, 169

Prized...146-148, 154-155, 166-167

Promised Land 32, 40

Redden, Dr. Ric...115

Relaxing 74

Rock Point 122, 126

Royal Charger...31-32

Ruhlmann 178, 183-184

Sakota, Naoki...199

San Felipe Handicap 87

Santa Anita..............................36, 51-52, 57-58, 65, 81, 83-85, 87-92, 96,
99-100, 147, 157, 161, 177-178

Santa Anita Derby 83, 85, 87, 89-90, 92, 96, 99-100

Saratoga 47, 70, 76, 133, 145, 149-150, 161, 193

Sekiguchi, Fusao...203

Shadai Farm......................................180, 192, 194, 196, 200-201

Shoemaker, Bill 61, 63-65, 85-86, 157

Skywalker...25-26, 39

Slew City Slew 163, 168-170

Spectacular Bid...130-131, 139

Stone Farm 6, 8-11, 18-21, 23, 26, 28, 41-43, 45, 50, 58,
80, 116, 134, 180, 189, 202, 205

Storm Cat...198

Straw, Phil and Becky..53

Strodes Creek...112, 203

Sullivan, Paul 12, 16, 22, 48-49

Sunday Silence................8-10, 23, 26, 28, 32, 40-51, 53-58, 61-69, 74-75,
79-82, 87-101, 103-111, 113-128, 132-138, 141-143, 145-149, 151-155,
159-192, 194-205

"Sunday Stop It" 63

Super Derby 151-154, 163

Swale 19, 89, 161

Swaps Stakes 33, 146, 152, 166

Tatham, Tom 24-28, 39-41, 43-44, 47-48, 80, 189, 203-204

Tayasu Tsuyoshi 196

Taylor, E.P. 27, 193

Temperate Sil 86-87

Tim Tam 110, 156

Tosmah...29

Travers Stakes...133, 149-150, 163

Triple Crown........29, 33, 42, 53, 67, 74, 83, 94, 102, 111, 113, 127-132, 138
141, 143, 145-147, 149, 163, 204

Understanding..8, 23, 32-33, 40

Valenzuela, A.C...156

Valenzuela, Pat 65-66, 68, 82, 87-88, 91-92, 104, 106-110,
123-126, 141-142, 147-148, 153, 156-160, 182, 184, 204

Wajima 192-193

Western Playboy..100, 106, 109, 167

Whittingham, Charlie.......9, 25, 44, 49-52, 56-69, 80-89, 91-93, 95-98, 101,
103-104, 109, 111-119, 125, 132-133, 136-137, 140-146, 148, 151, 153,
159-162, 165, 170, 172-175, 177-178, 181-184, 186-187, 189
190, 203-204

Whittingham, Peggy 109, 112, 137

Windfields 27, 30-31

Wishing Well.....................................6, 23, 26, 28, 32-40, 43-44, 47, 53, 56

Yoshida, Katsumi 199

Yoshida, Teruya 180, 196, 198-199, 203

Yoshida, Zenya 179-180, 190, 192, 195, 199, 201-202

Photo Credits

Cover photo: (Dan Johnson)

Page 1: Sunday Silence (Steve Stidham); Sunday Silence head shot (Candace Rushing)

Page 2: Halo (Joe Hickey); Hail to Reason (John C. Wyatt); Understanding (Bob Coglianese); Wishing Well and Sunday Silence (Courtesy of Arthur and Staci Hancock)

Page 3: Three Hancock generations (The Blood-Horse); Arthur Hancock (Anne M. Eberhardt); Hancocks with Sunday Silence (Tony Leonard)

Page 4: Tom Tatham (Anne M. Eberhardt); Ernest Gaillard (Steve Stidham); Charlie Whittingham with Sunday Silence (Four Footed Fotos)

Page 5: Patrick Valenzuela (Courtesy of Arthur and Staci Hancock); Chris McCarron and Whittingham (Four Footed Fotos)

Page 6: Houston and Sunday Silence (T. & T. Abahazy); Sunday Silence and Whittingham (The Blood-Horse)

Page 7: Sunday Silence winning the San Felipe; Winning the Santa Anita Derby; After Santa Anita Derby (all Four Footed Fotos)

Page 8-9: Winning the Kentucky Derby (Dan Johnson); Derby workout (*Lexington Herald-Leader*/Ron Garrison); Staci Hancock and Peggy Whittingham (E. Martin Jessee); Sunday Silence/Easy Goer at Preakness finish (Dan Johnson); Preakness stretch run, past the finish wire (both Skip Dickstein)

Page 10: Sunday Silence in Belmont paddock (Brant Gamma); Easy Goer winning the Belmont (The Blood-Horse)

Page 11: Prized winning the Swaps (Steve Stidham); Sunday Silence winning the Super Derby (Equine Sports Graphics); Winning the Breeders' Cup Classic (Jim Raftery)

Page 12: Sunday Silence working out (Steve Stidham); Teruya Yoshida, et al. (Shigeki Kikkawa)

Page 13: Winning the Californian (Shigeki Kikkawa); Criminal Type winning the Gold Cup (Steve Stidham)

Page 14: Stone Farm (Anne M. Eberhardt); Sunday Silence conformation (Tony Leonard)

Page 15: Hancock with Hall of Fame plaque (Courtesy of Arthur and Staci Hancock); Sunday Silence in Japan (both by Shigeki Kikkawa)

Page 16: Agnes Flight (Tomoya Moriuchi); Tayasu Tsuyoshi (Sankei Sports); Dance Partner (Sankei Sports)

ABOUT THE
AUTHOR

R ay Paulick is executive vice president and editorial director of The Blood-Horse, Inc. and editor-in-chief of its weekly flagship magazine, *The Blood-Horse*, which has provided Thoroughbred owners, breeders, and fans with racing news, analysis, statistics, and other vital information since 1916.

Paulick joined The Blood-Horse in 1992 as editor-in-chief. He also is editor of *TBH MarketWatch*, a twice-monthly newsletter for serious Thoroughbred investors, and he oversees the company's custom publishing division.

Before coming to *The Blood-Horse*, he was Midwest editor of the now-defunct *Racing Times* and managing editor of the *Thoroughbred Times*. From 1980 to 1988, he was a reporter for *Daily Racing Form* in Los Angeles.

Paulick resides in Lexington, Kentucky, with his wife, Carol, and two children.

Forthcoming titles
in the

THOROUGHBRED Legends ®

series:

Ruffian

Swaps

Affirmed and Alydar

Round Table

War Admiral

Available titles

Man o' War

Dr. Fager

Citation

Go for Wand

Seattle Slew

Forego

Native Dancer

Nashua

Spectacular Bid

John Henry

Personal Ensign